STANDARD
LOAN

UNLESS RECALLED BY ANOTHER READER
THIS ITEM MAY BE BORROWED FOR
FOUR WEEKS

To renew telephone:
01243 816089 (Bishop Otter)
01243 816099 (Bognor Regis)

WITHDRAWN

11.9.98

19. IAN 01.

26. NOV 03.

2 7 SEP 2007

Curriculum Change

The lessons of a decade

Edited by Maurice Galton

with contributions by
Pat D'Arcy
Jim Eggleston
Paul Hirst
Peter Kelly
David Tomley
Richard Whitfield

Leicester University Press

1980

First published in 1980 by Leicester University Press

Designed by Douglas Martin
Phototypeset in APS Saul
by Unwin Brothers Limited, The Gresham Press,
Old Woking, Surrey
A member of the Staples Printing Group

British Library Cataloguing in Publication Data
Curriculum change.
1. Curriculum planning – Great Britain
I. Galton, Maurice
375'.001'0941   LB1564.G7
ISBN 0 7185 1183 2

Contents

Introduction

In 1967 when Jack Kerr was appointed to a Chair of Education at Leicester University and titled his inaugural lecture 'The Problems of Curriculum Reform', it was in a sense an acknowledgment that the study of curriculum theory had become recognized in this country as a discipline in its own right. It was therefore appropriate that his lecture should be followed by four others in which the contributions of other educational disciplines to this new field of study were examined. These papers were eventually published as a book[1] and not the least useful of its functions was to provide students of curriculum theory with a number of American sources, since in that country a substantial amount of activity had taken place during the previous decade. Apart from Wheeler[2] this collection of papers continued to provide the only recognizable British source of writing on curriculum for students of education at both undergraduate and higher degree level until the publication of Lawrence Stenhouse's book.[3]

Professor Kerr retired in 1978. During the intervening decade the curriculum scene changed rapidly. A 'new wave' of curriculum theorists was born out of the experiences of those responsible for developing the Humanities Project[4] and the Integrated Studies Scheme[5] and introducing MACOS[6] into British schools. During this time there was growing evidence that, although the course content in schools and the nature of the terminal examination had changed considerably as the result of these new curriculum developments, there had been little change in teaching methods to accompany this renewal. The research emphasis therefore began to move away from problems of evaluation to that of curriculum dissemination and implementation. This was reflected in the awards made by grant-aiding bodies such as the Schools Council and the Nuffield Foundation, which in the early 1960s had been the main catalysts for much of the new development.

It seemed fitting, therefore, to mark the retirement of Professor Kerr by instituting a series of lectures bearing his name. It was also appropriate that most of the first contributors should have been associated in some way with Professor Kerr, which inevitably meant that they shared something of the same tradition of curriculum theory. Each lecturer was asked to look back over the previous decade and to take stock before the next round of renewal in the 1980s.

In order to shorten the time during which this volume was prepared it was decided to add a number of other papers to the present lectures, since only two lectures are given each year. As with the original Kerr volume no attempt was made to brief each contributor except in general terms with a mandate to look both backward and forward on the curriculum scene. All are agreed that the concepts advanced in the original Kerr lecture are important ones in providing a framework for the evaluation and implementation of new curricula. Each author, however, will have different views as to the extent to which an emphasis on this particular approach is possible within the context of different subject areas.

The papers are thus intended to encourage discussion rather than to provide definitive answers to specific curriculum problems. Professor Hirst defends the concept of rational curriculum planning in the light of some of the criticisms made by the 'new wave' theorists. In three succeeding papers, Professor Whitfield, David Tomley and Maurice Galton discuss the issues of *objectives*, *content* and *evaluation*, three of the corner-stones in the original model of the curriculum presented by Professor Kerr. Professor Kelly considers the problems of dissemination and implementation of new curricula, a subject which was largely overlooked in the approach of the curriculum theorists during the late 1960s.

Finally, two papers at the end of the book are each concerned to draw lessons from the failure of past developments. Professor Eggleston examines the history of curriculum renewal in science education and relates it to 'cycles of fashion' between heuristic and didactic models of teaching. Pat D'Arcy, who had the unusual experience of moving from a curriculum development project back into a school – most other developers in the 1960s moved to Universities or Colleges of Education – writes about her experiences as a teacher when trying to make use of recently introduced curriculum material.

Editing this book has been a privilege and a pleasure. Professor Kerr was known to all his colleagues and his students for his patience and kindness and for his penetrating and constructive criticisms. In dedicating this small volume of essays to him some of his friends are happy to acknowledge their debt.

M.G.

1. J. F. Kerr (ed.), *Changing the Curriculum* (1968).
2. D. K. Wheeler, *Curriculum Process* (1967).
3. L. Stenhouse, *An Introduction to Curriculum Research and Development* (1975).
4. *The Humanities Curriculum Project: An introduction* (1970).
5. *Schools Council Integrated Studies Project; Introduction* (1972).
6. *MAN: A course of study* (MACOS), Curriculum Development Association, Inc. (Washington, 1970).

1 The logic of curriculum development

PAUL HIRST

In the series of lectures springing from Professor Kerr's inaugural lecture in 1967, my own contribution discussed a number of ways in which philosophy could help curriculum planning.[1] Much of what I said was, directly or indirectly, a defence of certain principles underlying what is generally referred to as rational curriculum planning, rejecting at the same time certain particular doctrines with which the notion of rational planning got entangled under that heading. I was in fact defending rational curriculum planning against a particular doctrinaire expression of it by its extreme supporters. Returning 12 years later to join in a second series of lectures in honour of Jack Kerr, I want to pick up my previous theme in the light of what has happened in the last 12 years in curriculum studies. I am still a firm defender of what I see to be the basic principles of rational curriculum planning but now it is a case of a straight defence of these against the misunderstandings and, as I see it, errors of various opponents. Nothing has weakened my conviction about the importance of the fundamental principles, but certainly I think all that has happened has led to a sharper grasp of what those principles do and do not imply and how they are to be applied in concrete situations. I want therefore to re-assert the central tenets of rational curriculum planning as I see them and to comment on their significance for curriculum development.

The major principles I wish to re-assert stem from the very definition of a curriculum that I gave 12 years ago: 'a programme of activities (by teachers and pupils) designed so that pupils will attain as far as possible certain educational ends or objectives'.[2] I want to make four points that follow from this. First, in curriculum decisions we are concerned with a programme of intentional, deliberately and consciously planned activities. A curriculum consists of intentionally undertaken activities – necessarily so. Secondly, enshrined in the definition is the notion that these activities are planned so that certain objectives will be reached, so that the pupils will come to know certain things, have certain skills, will be able to appreciate certain things, have certain habits, patterns of emotional response and so on. A curriculum therefore necessarily has objectives. Thirdly, curriculum activities are planned as the means whereby these objectives are reached. They are the means to the intended ends. Teaching and learning are the names of these activities. Fourthly, a curriculum is only rationally defensible insofar as (a) we can justify the choice of objectives, and (b) we can justify the means adopted for reaching those ends. Now each of these four points has been directly challenged and from the challenges much of profit has emerged.

First, the idea that a curriculum consists of deliberately, consciously planned activities. Surely, it is often argued, much that goes on in schools and much that is most valuable happens without conscious planning. Ought we not therefore to think of the curriculum as providing opportunities for things to happen, for children to grow, to realize themselves, to determine what they will do? My reply to that is simply this. Human institutions like schools are what men make them, they are not natural phenomena. Men give them their purposes. We can and do have institutions where children determine their own activities and their value I do not dispute. But it seems to me confusing to see institutions of that kind as having curricula. If it is desirable to have institutions which deliberately 'plan programmes of activities to bring about pupils' learning', and I personally judge that to be highly desirable, we really do need a term for what those institutions systematically organize. The traditional term is 'curriculum' and I see much to be lost and nothing gained by stretching the meaning of the term to cover quite other enterprises. Even to stretch the term 'curriculum' to cover the hidden, implicit or unconscious sequence of learning what goes on when pupils follow a consciously planned curriculum can be seriously misleading. The phrase 'hidden curriculum' has the value of a paradox in that it alerts us to attend consciously to matters otherwise unacknowledged in our planning. But that being said, we should, I think, recognize that we need a term limited to what we do consciously plan if confusions are to be avoided and I am unrepentant in believing that 'curriculum' is best used for that purpose.

Second, it has been argued that a curriculum does not necessarily have objectives. There may not necessarily be specifiable ends or achievements to which a curriculum is directed. This objection has been supported on a number of different grounds. It has, for instance, been insisted that the outcome of education in the arts cannot be specified beforehand. Sometimes it is claimed that the desired achievements are of their nature unspecifiable, sometimes that the specification of objectives reduces the achievements aimed at to the crudest level of work. Again it has been argued that specifying objectives restricts teaching so that it is unresponsive to immediate opportunities for learning. Others have seen the formulation of agreed objectives as a quite misleading exercise, it being really the case that under the agreed formulae lie major disagreements about what is going on. And yet again this whole approach through objectives has been pronounced unworkable because even given a set of objectives we cannot effectively plan to make sure we achieve them.[3]

My reaction to this kind of catalogue of supposed objections is that these attacks simply miss their target. They show a lack of appreciation of what is really being said about objectives. The necessity for objectives is simply the necessity for us to know what it is we want children to learn if we are to do our best to help them learn it. Pupils must learn something, and how can we plan that they achieve that without being clear what it is? Put another way, all teaching is necessarily the teaching of something. This kind of intentional activity by teachers must, logically must, have an end which it seeks. But that is not to demand that children make the same thing in art, nor is it to be inflexible in one's planning or conduct of activities. Nor is it to say that the objectives can be articulated in any one crude way. What is needed is that teachers know what is to be learnt sufficiently specifically to be able to know when that is being achieved and when not. Some objectives may not be expressible in statements but only be capable of being indicated or being recognized in terms of general criteria. Nor is the notion of objectives in any way tied to any claim about the necessary effectiveness of the means taken to these ends. It is simply the general insistence that if we are even to try to bring about learning we must know what it is we want pupils to learn.

The real evils that have become associated with the notion of objectives have arisen from the doctrines of behaviouristic psychology that some devotees have insisted on. Of course, if you insist that the outcomes of the curriculum must be particlar forms of overt behaviour, the criticisms of reductionism, for example, will be valid. But if, in getting away from the dogmatic insistence on having behavioural objectives, we do away with all objectives, we are inevitably in deep trouble in all curriculum planning. We can then never be rational about curriculum development for we have not got a curriculum to be rational about.

It is an interesting exercise to see how far those who advocate some other, objectiveless characterization of a curriculum do in fact get away from the notion of objectives whilst expressing themselves adequately about the enterprise. Insofar as I understand Professor Lawrence Stenhouse's 'process model',[4] it seems to me that all he says presupposes the existence of objectives. Indeed I think that not at all surprising, for if curriculum processes are those of teaching and learning, they cannot be demarcated from other processes except in terms of their objectives. When Professor Stenhouse gets down to the detail of curriculum planning in the humanities, it is quite clear that he has specifiable objectives. He may wish to elaborate at great length the teaching process he advocates, but his concern for, say, 'procedural neutrality' is surely nothing but a concern for processes that are not distinguishable apart from the kinds of results that are aimed at, i.e. objectives of certain kinds. What is at stake is not really whether there are objectives for a curriculum, but what sort of things these are. Once it is recognized that these may be of many different kinds, and not just items of overt behaviour, but concepts, attitudes, skills, creative capacities, achievements characterized by virtue of certain principles, etc., all of which must be pursued according to their distinctive natures, all seemingly valid objections to the idea of objectives are I think dissipated. Of course the evidence that pupils have or have not achieved a set of objectives must be behavioural, but that is another matter. The central point remains crucial. Unless we are concerned with certain objectives for teaching and learning, the object of our concern is not a curriculum. To fail to be explicit about objectives is to approach a curriculum inadequately.

Third, with the attack there has been on the necessity for objectives has gone an attack on the notion that the curriculum consists of the means planned for reaching the objectives. The rejection of a means-ends connection here is sometimes forcefully put as an attack on the idea that a school curriculum is like an industrial production line. The child comes as the raw material and ends up like a car manufactured through a process of engineering. That indeed is to see the curriculum as the means to certain ends. Of course, the analogy seems most apt in terms of processes beloved of behavioural psychologists once more. But attacking this one form of means-ends processing is not to attack the idea that a curriculum is a means-ends process of some other kind. If the ends are forms of human understanding, creative capacities, moral dispositions and so on, the processes for achieving these will not be like those of a car production line. But so what? Teaching is not like engineering and concepts are not like ball bearings. None of that alters the fact that the rational planning of motor car production is means-ends, and so is the rational planning of producing human beings with certain qualities who are, say, capable of scientific understanding or of moral conduct. What we need to know is the character of the activities that can lead to these kinds of human achievement and to plan for these. Because of the differing nature of the ends, the relationship of means to ends will take on a different character too. It will not be that of a causal sequence as in the manufacture of physical objects certainly. What the relationship is we need to discover in its own right.[5]

These three points lead I think to a fourth, that if it is a rationally planned curriculum we are after, if we want a defensible curriculum, we must see that we can defend (a) the objectives at which it aims, and (b) the processes as means for achieving those objectives. But, you will recall, this has been objected to as simply completely unrealizable, a totally impracticable demand. In the first place it is argued that we have not got an appropriate way of setting out all the objectives and of then making a rational choice amongst them. The whole thing is surely much too vast and unmanageable an enterprise to settle rationally. In the second place, even if we could settle the objectives, we simply could not produce a coherent plan that was the most defensible means of teaching and learning to achieve these ends. In terms of both ends and means the whole thing seems like a megalomaniac's nightmare, a sort of philosopher's dream of a rational world which bears no relationship to the real situation. Certainly it does not represent anything we ever do in practice. True, particularly in the U.S.A., attempts have been made to do this vast job in behavioural terms. But none of these has been able to carry the job through in a fully defensible, rational way. What then are we to say to this attack which has the effect of making the whole approach of rational curriculum planning look irrelevant?

The major reply to this charge of impracticability is that it totally misrepresents the significance of the principles that assert the necessity for objectives and means-ends planning. The principles assert the *logic* of rational curriculum planning. They state that a curriculum is defensible only within these terms and only to the extent that these principles are met. Insofar as they set out a sequence, it is a sequence that an argument purporting to give justification must satisfy. It is not, and must never be confused with, a temporal sequence for planning, nor is it a planning methodology. It is not an assertion that in planning you must determine and justify all your objectives before attending to any consideration of means. That would be a practical nonsense. To select certain objectives rationally demands a knowledge that possible methods for reaching them exist. The two must be considered in relation to each other. New methods may suggest new objectives. But in the end, wherever the ideas come from and in whatever sequence, we have to produce any defence that is to be valid according to this means-to-ends pattern. The distinction between the logic of rational curriculum planning and the methodology of rational curriculum planning or rational curriculum development is a form of the distinction between 'the logical' and 'the psychological' long familiar to philosophers of education.[6] The logic of an argument is the structure that guarantees its validity. But that argument may be constructed in many different ways psychologically. If this means-ends model is that of the logic of rational curriculum planning, what it says is that insofar as your curriculum is justifiable in this framework it is rationally defensible. It is then another question as to how far any curriculum is so defensible. Because we may not in principle or in practice be able to defend the whole of a curriculum, that is no reason why we should not progressively seek to produce one that is slowly becoming more defensible.

That leads to a second reply to the attack on the practicality of this approach. Built into this criticism of rational curriculum planning is a complete mistake about the application of this logic of planning. Not only is it falsely taken to be an expression of planning methodology, it is also taken for granted that rational curriculum planning must be grand-scale or Utopian and *carte blanche* or *ab initio*. It is assumed that rational curriculum planning demands planning from scratch and the implementation of what we can thus first defend. True there have not been wanting those, often philosophers, who at the drop of a hat would set about planning a curriculum in these terms. Plato's *Republic* is a magnificent example showing someone attempting just this approach. But rational planning does not have to be Utopian in this sense and indeed I think it is an irrational application of the logic.

Karl Popper in *The Open Society and Its Enemies* argued very forcefully that rational social engineering (and that includes for my purpose rational curriculum planning) should be piecemeal and not Utopian.[7] Utopian engineering he outlines as the settling of our ultimate ends first of all in the belief that without that our intermediate ends, being really only means to the ultimate ends, will be ill considered and not rationally defensible. We thus need for all engineering a blueprint of our ultimate ends. Piecemeal engineering on the other hand may or may not be backed by some Utopian ideal or blueprint. It is more concerned with searching out and overcoming the most urgent existing deficiencies, rather than searching out and fighting for the overall, ultimate good. Present deficiences can be relatively easily established. It is inevitably more difficult to justify rationally what ought to be done as an ultimate ideal when so much is at stake. What is more, starting from an ideal blueprint it is well nigh impossible to judge its practicality, what the means to it are, what negative results might come about and therefore how far in practice there would be real improvement. With piecemeal engineering the damage is not very great if things go wrong and re-adjustment is not very difficult. Both ends and means can be more easily argued out rationally and without so much distortion by emotional factors. Reasonable compromise is possible where there are disagreements and genuine disagreement there so often is. Utopian engineering because of its vast implications needs high autocratic control to carry it through in face of many who see the situation more locally and in shorter term, for the possibilities of success depend on holding the situation stable for some long time for large changes to be made.

All these points about social changes in general seem to me to apply most pertinently to the curriculum context. But let me spell out in more specific terms some of their significance for curriculum planning. To elaborate a defensible ideal and the means to it necessitates a vast amount of knowledge and understanding of men and society that we simply do not have. A quick glance at Plato shows how his Utopianism comes unstuck on this score. What relevant knowledge we have is to be found in such disciplines as, say, philosophy, psychology and sociology. But these are all disparate understandings of aspects of human life, dependent on partial abstractions. That such an array of disciplines can ever, in principle, provide in an appropriate form the understanding we need to judge of ultimate ends or of means to them is far from obvious. Certainly right now they are totally inadequate. Each is extremely limited in what it studies and each is an area of controversy rather than of agreed rational conclusions. And again, without far more understanding than we begin to have, how could we begin to control affairs so as actually to achieve what might be planned? Working in Utopian fashion, planning from scratch using existing theory to formulate ends and deriving our practice from those, the whole enterprise is doomed as a rational procedure for determining a curriculum. If we are to have a rationally defensible curriculum we must therefore approach things in another way.

Whether we like it or not, we have to take decisions on the basis of the best knowledge and understanding available to us. But that knowledge is not, and I think cannot, all be made fully explicit and consciously attended to directly. We must make our decisions on a great deal of tacit, implicit understanding that is the product of much practical experience which has been gained in the context of doing particular tasks. We decide matters like this because we cannot work from a comprehensive set of fundamental considerations. We act out of what might be called the 'common sense' of this area of experience, an understanding built up over a long period of time often in pragmatic terms. It is necessarily acquired within a social tradition and in existing institutions by engaging in the relevant activities in an enlightened and informed way. This wisdom, insight, understanding, is only in part articulated and in principle I doubt if it ever can be fully articulated. Insofar as it is articulated it can be rationally scrutinized, indefensible beliefs and inadequate ideas being replaced by more adequately justified elements. What the disciplines do for educational practice is surely to enable us to refine this 'common-sense' base from which we determine what to do, making it progressively more defensible and our actions more justifiable as a result. Yet this is to say that our curriculum decisions are justifiable only by appeal to this sophisticated 'common sense' and not by a direct appeal to the disciplines alone. Educational practice that rests on appeals to the disciplines directly and alone will inevitably be dangerously ill-considered. Yet the disciplines are the systematic means we have for advancing the 'common-sense' basis on which rational decisions can be made. The disciplines alone can provide well-founded corrections to the philosophical, psychological, sociological and other beliefs that permeate our 'common-sense'. New disciplines may arise of course, but it is only by progress in old and new disciplines which are abstractions from 'common-sense' that the latter can become more rational. I see no reason to believe a unified theory of educational practice is possible when any generalizing theory must of its nature be a partial abstraction from the realities of practice.

What then does rational curriculum development in piecemeal terms involve? First, it means a rejection of seeking a Utopian total curriculum plan derived from the disciplines and then forced onto the practical context. Instead it means looking for ways in which we can seriously hope to improve on what we do because the deficiencies in our practice are right there for us to see using the best 'sophisticated common-sense' that we have available. Popper has pointed out that even in the much simpler world of mechanical engineering, large-scale blueprints for machines are not derived straight from pure theory and fundamental research. They are instead based on experiments of a trial and error kind and many small improvements. 'The wholesale and large scale method works only where piecemeal method has furnished us first with a great number of detailed experiences and even then only within the sector of these experiences.'[8] But if we must progress through small-scale new curriculum developments, these must indeed be based on truly informed 'common-sense' and assessed as rational developments. What the inspiration generating new developments may be will vary. Whether there is a methodology for planning new experiments so that the results are likely to be more readily defensible rationally, I am not at all sure. But if we are ever to move forward rationally, small-scale experiments must be critically evaluated so that ever more defensible decisions can be made in the future. What sort of appraisal that involves is therefore a crucial question.

If I am right in what I have argued, it means evaluating small-scale experiments in terms of the objectives and then the means to those ends. If rational curriculum planning has a means-ends logic, appraisal must be in those terms. But what does that involve more specifically? It means experimenting with particular objectives in mind chosen for clear reasons in the light of our existing 'sophisticated common-sense' knowledge of the situation and with deliberately chosen means based on the best evidence we have. We must then investigate the actual events and their consequences, unintended as well as intended. The point is to see both what happened in practice and why it happened. We need an explanation of what happened in terms of why people did what they did. That is, an explanation in terms of the human decisions in the event, one of reasons as well as causes. This enquiry must involve a great deal of evidence from the direct participants, both teachers and pupils, as much as from observers. Understanding what happened and why will involve many complex and very different elements that I do not think can be given in any one integrated account. What happened is truly no one thing and we must get used to the idea of combining together evaluations which are necessarily partial and from different points of view. Such multiple evaluations involve the use of the disciplines and areas of enquiry that are at present less sophisticated. But we need to think of these as leading to the making of better practical judgments as to what ought to be done in future in this area of the curriculum. Such judgments can, of course, only be responsibly made if the results of the evaluations are drawn into the whole pool of 'common-sense' so making its deliberations more rational. In this way we can progress from the evaluations of an experiment to new practical policy conclusions. Formulating explanations of what happened, even from many points of view, is valuable in curriculum development only insofar as it leads to better practical decisions.

Seen in this way, much curriculum experiment is of very limited, if any, value in advancing rational curriculum development. To begin with it is often not conceived in adequate means-ends terms: it is inadequately conceived as an experiment that can lead to more justifiable practical policies. But in the second place, if it is evaluated it is frequently evaluated in ways that fail to provide the explanations needed to sophisticate our educational common-sense. If the experiment and the evaluation both ignore or evade the logic of rational curriculum planning it is not surprising that we waste a great deal of time, energy and money – not to mention the educational harm we sometimes do in the process. In responsible evaluation we shall certainly use traditional quantification methods for all the understanding they can provide. To ignore the full range of experience and expertise developed in the existing social sciences must be absurd when, in the curriculum area, we are after precisely the kinds of understanding that are their concerns, partial though these are. But the newer forms of evaluation, often classed together under the label 'illuminative', are at least as important provided they are conducted in the pursuit of rational explanations of what happened. And that qualification is crucial. Case studies using portrayal techniques for instance have much to tell us that cannot be acquired by other means. But only if it is recognized (a) that such studies are of necessity intensely theory-loaded, (b) that these techniques are as partial and abstracting as other techniques, (c) that the concepts and categories used need to be used with the production of generalizations in mind, and (d) that the aim is to explain.

The upshot of evaluation, I have maintained, must be a new determination of what ought to be done in future, based not on evaluation exercises in abstraction, but those seen as improving our stock of practical wisdom. Our educational 'common-sense', sophisticated by the evaluation of experiments, can then produce progressively refined practical judgments, progressively more rationally defensible decisions. These can only be expressed in principles for practice, and these are necessarily general statements that refer to situations only insofar as they share common features. Curriculum theory I see as aiming at the production of such general principles for our practice, the best, most rationally defensible statements of what we ought to do in situations having certain characteristics. Yet such principles have to be applied in individual contexts and that can be done only by those within the context. Rational curriculum development therefore demands that those taking decisions be able to use general principles intelligently. They must from their own sophisticated 'common-sense' be able to judge the applicability of the principles. Maybe sometimes general principles are of little use. The explanatory understanding achieved in various forms of evaluation in other experiments may be the most help. How best one trains teachers in making the best judgments for rational curriculum development in their own contexts is an issue I cannot go into here. As an ideal one might like to think of every teacher engaging in his own rational experimentation and evaluation along the lines I have suggested. But I suspect that is, in the end, as irrational and megalomaniac an idea as the Utopianism I earlier rejected. We need teachers who can indeed make rational practical judgments in their own contexts, but that is surely only possible in general if there is a body of rational curriculum principles they can intelligently employ. In curriculum affairs, as in life in general, we cannot hope to determine rationally what to do without a body of general principles that enshrine the most defensible practice granted certain conditions.

I have tried to give an account of what I now consider rational curriculum development to involve. To my mind two things now stand out much more clearly than they did when I lectured here on this topic 12 years ago. First, the objectives and means-ends account of rational curriculum planning must be seen as an expression of the logic of planning and development, not an expression of a methodology. Second, that logic must be used in piecemeal, not Utopian, attempts to rationally develop curricula rationally. We are now, I think, at the exciting stage of trying to discover what the application of this logic really means in serious experimentation. If we can keep our heads and hang on to the logic of the business in the midst of a welter of new ideas for practice and for evaluation, we might before long actually begin to build a more substantial body of defensible curriculum principles. Heaven knows we need that.

1. P. H. Hirst, 'The contribution of philosophy to the study of the curriculum', in J. F. Kerr (ed.), *Changing the Curriculum* (1968).
2. *Ibid.*, 40.
3. For a useful outline and discussion of these and other objections, see L. Stenhouse, *An Introduction to Curriculum Research and Development* (1975).
4. *Ibid.*, ch. 7.
5. See discussion of means-ends relationships in H. Sockett, *Designing the Curriculum* (1976).
6. See my paper, 'The logical and psychological aspects of teaching a subject', in P. H. Hirst, *Knowledge and the Curriculum* (1974).
7. See K. R. Popper, *The Open Society and its Enemies* (1945), especially vol. 1, ch. 9.
8. *Ibid.*, 158.

2 Curriculum objectives: help or hindrance?

RICHARD WHITFIELD

I first met Jack Kerr in 1964 while serving as a school science teacher. Having applied to do the Leicester M.Ed. I had an admission interview with him during which he gave my tentative research ideas a critical scrutiny. Yes, he would seriously consider me for supervision provided I structured my curriculum evaluation outline rather more carefully after digesting Bloom's *Taxonomy of Educational Objectives*,[1] and what a mouthful that seemed to be! My training as a physical scientist, containing no biology (such travesties of curricular imbalance continue to be perpetuated), did not immediately inform me that the work of Bloom and his co-workers was simply an attempt to classify outcome behaviours of students in an approximate hierarchy which was not contingent upon the substantive content of the psychological operations.

At that time only the first volume (cognitive domain) of Bloom had crossed the Atlantic, but it was to be my first introduction to the field of curriculum design and evaluation and, once deciphered from the jargon which educational theorists seemed intent on using, it was to change fundamentally my approach to both lesson planning and student assessment in school and later in university. It had been all too easy to teach with the apparent acclaim of peers and superiors and even the appreciation of pupils without giving much, if any, real attention to reasons why, to intentions, motives, goals, aims, objectives and all such related concepts. Here were these pupils in my charge for chemistry, physics and divinity lessons; here were some syllabuses in varied detail, more often than not based upon our internal modifications to external examination prescriptions, and the pupils' future in employment and higher and further education was crucially dependent upon, as one colleague vividly put it, their 'being caused to pass' the external hurdles. So the task boiled down quite simply to promoting the required achievements through high teacher expectations and demand on pupils, through thorough lesson preparation and assignment marking, while making the process for both parties in the engagement as enjoyable as possible, yet recognizing that discipline, graft and a degree of mutual pain seemed inevitable! And so, one surmises, it remains the case in many classrooms at every level of the educational system: learning, often of a very sophisticated character, is caused without the identification by the teacher of a series of curriculum objectives framed in a manner which would win the approval of educationists who write and lecture about such matters.

So are 'educational objectives' just another item within educational theory which in the execution of teaching generally become redundant, or do they form the foundation stone for effective professional practice and evaluation? In this paper I shall argue the latter, while recognizing that some practitioners may teach effectively without an intensive analysis of their goals, provided others have at some stage supplied a framework for their activities with its own implicit educational aims. Space however does not allow an exhaustive treatment of this topic and for further detail readers are referred to appropriate sections and references in the relatively recent books by Davies[2] and Stenhouse[3], which from somewhat different tenets cover the topic quite adequately, including the debates for and against the use of objectives in curriculum design.

TEACHING AS INTENTIONAL ACTIVITY

During their professional engagement teachers practise many different activities. A science teacher might, for example, be seen writing on the blackboard, or demonstrating an experiment, asking questions or making statements about science, correcting a pupil's misunderstanding, marking books, or giving practical instructions; the same teacher might on the other hand be talking to the laboratory steward, reading an apparatus catalogue, sweeping up broken glass, repairing some apparatus, signing a register, or stopping a fight between pupils. We tend to associate the first group of activities with *teaching* science, even though the others can form part of the legitimate activities of a science teacher. If we examine possible pupil activities during a science lesson, we may distinguish some which are more characteristic than others of pupils *learning* science. The former might include discussing a scientific problem, performing practical work, reading a textbook, making notes, asking questions, or doing test questions. The latter might include daydreaming, putting chalk down bunsen burners, discussing a football match, tidying the laboratory, or doing history homework.

These apparent demarcations between activities must however be viewed with some caution since if, for example, the teacher is writing in error on the blackboard it would be odd to conclude that science was being taught. Similarly, if a pupil's question is simply whether he may open a window, it would be difficult to conclude that he was learning science. The examples thus serve to indicate that neither teaching nor learning can be described by kinds of activities easily identified when divorced from their specific context. Eating and drinking can be described in that way, but teaching and learning cannot. They are 'polymorphous' activities[4] like working, or playing, or loving.

To understand what teaching is, we must search for a distinguishing feature of those activities which we associate directly with it. In this respect, the crucial question is: '*Why* is the teacher doing the activity under scrutiny, and what is his or her implicit aim?' This question seeks to search out the teacher's *intentions* when deciding to ask a scientific question, write on the blackboard, or mark the books. The distinguishing feature of specifically teaching activities is that they are activities performed with the intention that the students will learn something educationally valuable. The other activities – stopping the fight, signing the register, and so on – will in general not carry that specific intention or aim, though stopping the fight may provide the teacher with an unplanned opportunity for social and moral education.

So we may say that we are teaching if we lay on a series of activities, the *aim* of which is that pupils shall learn something educationally justifiable. This statement may seem to be obvious in the extreme, but a vital deduction arises from it. This is that teaching is contingent upon the teacher having aims or intentions connected with pupils' learning. In fact, teaching is logically characterized more by its intentions than its activities. One may develop competence in all manner of activities – all those overt, visible things which we associate with teaching, but all this *could* be of little consequence if we neglect to develop a fundamental framework of *aims* which form the basis for guiding, selecting, and structuring the activities in which we engage in the classroom. Aims in teaching are rarely visible in the classroom; they can only usually be inferred from the visible activity, but they are the ultimate justification for any teaching act. Whatever else a teacher may be employed for, it is to have intentions of a fairly specific kind concerned with pupils learning something which is valued by the teacher and/or his professional colleagues and/or the wider community. We cannot be said to be teaching without having aims, whether thought out by ourselves or by others, and if we have too hazy a notion about these we may be led into all kinds of misguided 'teaching' acts. One may without one's own aims become a competent technician carrying out orders devised by others, but the autonomous professional teacher thinks through his or her own.

This analysis thus stresses the teacher's necessary role as manager of pupils' intended learning; it stresses the necessary distinction between the teacher as an authority and the pupils as persons being initiated into what is for them a new realm of knowledge and understanding. This does not deny that pupils can have their own aims concerned with learning, nor does it deny that pupils can sometimes engage in worthwhile learning when the teacher does not deliberately intend it, under relatively random conditions. The description merely draws attention to the fact that our concept of teaching and our provision of special institutions in which this activity can go on necessarily presumes that much of learning can and should be made more than a random business. But planning for learning presupposes intentional teaching, and this logically requires teachers to have aims or intentions for pupils in connection with some valued area or object of experience.

AIMS, OBJECTIVES AND BEHAVIOURAL OBJECTIVES

The distinction has often been drawn in the literature that educational *aims* serve to suggest the general directions in which overall curricula and their constituent courses may be steered. For example a whole curriculum may have general educational or specialized academic or vocational aims which have implications for particular elements within it. However, such global aims do not and cannot incorporate any relative valuations which teachers may have arising from their specific task in a specific set of institutional circumstances. At times, certain aims may be seen to be in competition with each other, or even mutually exclusive, as for example when a teacher wishes to foster an enquiry approach to science or history so that students can develop a wide range of skills while, concurrently, the vocational aspirations of the pupils require them to pass an external examination which may be based upon an overloaded syllabus and which samples a restricted range of intellectual qualities. Teachers are rarely able to select their aims in the absence of the more obvious constraints of space, time and equipment available, and so on, and in practice operational aims are a complex of the teacher's valuations and priorities and the contextual parameters which may or may not be under his control. But in every situation the teacher cannot avoid the professional responsibility of grappling with these factors which necessarily form the basis for his teaching intentions on a macro- (e.g. overall work scheme planning) or micro- (e.g. within-lesson decision) scale.

Educational *objectives*, insofar as they are distinguished from aims are concerned with the more precise outcomes from a particular course of teaching, or even a single lesson. Some examples will serve to make this distinction clear.

Examples of general aims
1 To interest pupils in local history.
2 To develop inquiring minds.
3 To help pupils to see craftwork in relation to the rest of culture.
4 To prepare some pupils for careers in science.
5 To help pupils to solve mathematics problems.

Examples of objectives
1 To develop the ability to formulate historical hypotheses.
2 To foster the ability to interconvert data in tabular and graphical forms.
3 To develop skill in mixing water colours.
4 To increase pupils' ability to work as a team in sharing out a complex task.
5 To develop an interest in laboratory safety.

There is however a further distinction to be made concerning the concept of *behavioural objectives*; these are the overt, visible, and hence potentially quantifiable, changes in student 'thinking', 'feeling' and 'acting' behaviour which teachers hope to bring about. Behavioural objectives emphasize the learner's overt achievements, rather than the somewhat intangible qualities of mind such as 'understanding'. This further distinction is based on one of the more tenable aspects of a behaviourist view of learning, namely, that whatever changes go on in a person's mind as a result of learning, we can only infer them by looking at what he *does* afterwards which he did not do before. (Of course, 'does' is not confined to manipulative skills, but includes for example new kinds of reasoning, and actions which suggest new attitudes.) Much unnecessary educational controversy surrounds the notion of behavioural objectives.[5] Avid opponents of behaviourism fear that if teachers toy with behavioural objectives they *prespecify* the individual responses of pupils in their care. This is clearly dangerous for it makes teaching more akin either to indoctrination – an activity through which it becomes impossible for the learner to question the expected response he makes in the learning situation – or to a learning production line which is insufficiently flexible to take into account individual differences in time and place. Extreme behaviourists, on the other hand, seeking to ascribe all human learning to simplistic stimulus-response theory, wish to eradicate from schooling all those teacher intentions which cannot be measured quantitatively. More appropriately, however, 'behavioural objectives' serve to *indicate the kinds* of behaviour characteristic of some learner end-states, rather than *prescribe the specific* terminal behaviours to be brought about through teaching.

Teaching objectives thus become inseparable from the achievement of certain kinds of pupil end-states in relation to a body of content. An example of a general behavioural objective or outcome in relation to a course of study might be 'the ability to apply previous scientific understanding to new situations'; a parallel example of a specific behavioural objective in relation to a lesson or a series of test questions* would be

---

*Valid tests and examinations should test the skills and qualities which the teaching course seeks to foster.

'the ability to apply various methods of separating and purifying chemicals to the demands of an astronaut's life support system in a space craft'. In teaching, many of our aims can be translated into recognizable kinds of pupil behaviour, as several of the more recent curriculum development projects illustrate, but it would be naive to assume that all are susceptible of precise description, especially in the realm of attitudes and values, let alone of measurement in meaningful quantitative terms.

The practical chain for the isolation of teaching objectives may be shown as follows:

Justifications for teaching X in an educational setting:

    ↓ suggest

Aims for teaching X

    ↓ translation and selection gives:

Objectives of particular courses ✝ in X

    ↓ by selecting and relating these to
    specific content and teaching
    strategies/methods we obtain:

Objectives for particular lessons ✝ in X

✝ Some of these at least are amenable to behavioural specification; i.e. identifiable in terms of observable qualities of pupils.

SOURCES AND CLASSES OF OBJECTIVES

This chain indicates that objectives should originate from justifications regarding their educational value, for which there are essentially three major sources: society, individual students, and our cultural inheritance. Here is not the place to go into the different demands which each of these three prime sources of educational objectives may be justified in making upon the curriculum for different age and ability levels. However, as far as much of school education is concerned I have argued elsewhere,[6] as have other authors, that our cultural inheritance, distilled through various modes of conscious awareness, has a logically prior claim upon curriculum priorities compared with the other two sources. It is nonetheless readily possible to devise classes of objectives derivative from each major source.

The Bloom taxonomy can, from one perspective, be said to be an attempt to classify the spectrum of human abilities in student-centred terms, while classifications within the map of Man's knowledge and understanding, such as those of Hirst[7] and Phenix,[8] provide the substantive structures through which these abilities may be developed. One example of a society-focussed objectives map is that of Derr,[9] and with the renewed contemporary emphasis upon the social accountability of education,[10] such classes of demand upon the educational system to sustain and renew 'the hand which feeds it' seem likely to gain in prominence. It seems clear that only with adequate analyses of the claims of often competing aims can we look ahead to a more justified spectrum of curriculum priorities with which both the wider community and the teaching profession can be satisfied.

Yet while classes of objectives can clarify, they may also confuse and even distract, particularly if they become too numerous or extensive in content. A list of 50 objectives expressed in precise behavioural terms may be useful for a training manual concerned with the effective operation of a piece of technological equipment, but would hardly help in the daily planning of mathematics or geography lessons. It is arguable that no teacher can 'bear in mind' more than about five distinctive objectives at any time during the execution of teaching, and, as has been implied, the point at which objectives perhaps have most use is in pre-lesson planning and post-lesson evaluation. Lists of objectives remain barren and lifeless without human activities and materials which illustrate them, and there are limits to the number of objectives which may be seriously pursued in an educational (cf. training) programme.

CONSEQUENCES AND PROCESSES OF ISOLATING OBJECTIVES

It is of course a pointless exercise to isolate objectives, through which value judgments become clarified, without an operational commitment to them; once listed they should not be forgotten, for a programme of work, or indeed a whole institution, can only 'provide' in terms of the aims it adopts. The immediate benefits of identifying aims or objectives are (a) to give the curriculum tasks a focus and direction, (b) to provide guidance on the selection of both lesson content and teaching strategies, and (c) to make it possible validly to gauge the results of the teaching process. Without objectives the vast range of possible content and tactics for the educational encounter have no filter, that is no selection criteria, and this can lead to a misuse of curriculum time, to a wastage of potential student talent, to a warping of minds and a crippling of the imagination. Because many of our more traditional tests and examinations have not been explicitly related to curriculum objectives, they have not only been technically invalid, but have exerted feedback on the teaching process of a kind which conflicts with professional values. Aims, means, and the assessment of ends must be closely and realistically interlocked within curriculum design, and none of these three elements should over-ride another.[11]

Some of those who oppose the use of objectives as part of the map of curriculum design do so on the erroneous assumption that the rational *procedural* order of (1) objectives — (2) learning experiences — (3) evaluation of attainment of objectives is being prescribed and that an analysis of valued educational *processes* is being denied in favour of armchair prescription and prespecification. While *some* objectives may be derived from analysis remote from the action of teaching and learning, most emerge (and certainly in much curriculum development) from an examination of professional practice[12] which can thus incorporate important issues of appropriateness, feasibility and motivation.

Take, for example, an apparently non-analytical teacher of literature who is known to succeed in developing a love of poetry in many of his pupils. His overall aim may be quite simply to encourage his pupils to 'like poetry'; but if we analyse his lessons we shall discover not only at least some of the discrete behaviours of pupils through which they display their love of poetry, which thus articulate somewhat more precisely his intentions, but we will also have objectives suggested through the richness of the learning experiences which the teacher is providing. We may even find that pupils from time to time scan and measure poetry, write a précis of it, and assemble facts of poets' lives, and that these perhaps mundane behaviours are of comparable importance to 'creative writing' and 'dramatization' in developing interest and commitment. Hence the analysis of manifestly enjoyable and worthwhile teaching/learning activities is an important source of inferred objectives; teacher group 'brainstorming' is another. Curricular design procedures do not necessarily have to follow the logic of a model; curricular models cannot in any case indicate fully the interactions between their constituent elements.

EXAMPLES OF OBJECTIVES IN USE

A glance at the local and national curriculum and examination development literature in the UK readily shows us that now, compared with 10 or 15 years ago, educational aims and objectives have become a part of the expected currency, despite the admitted problems and dangers of their indiscriminate use. They have found, perhaps not surprisingly, a central place in the training literature of the Manpower Services Commission, the Technician and Business Education Councils, and professional bodies such as the Chartered Society of Physiotherapy. Medical educators have used the concept more widely than their teacher education counterparts, and the C.N.A.A. requires adequate attention to objectives in all its course submissions even though this cannot guarantee by any means the day-by-day utilization of the objectives concept by the teaching staffs of the submitting institutions. As has been implied, lists of objectives can be 'paper dragons', the 'Science 5–13' project[13] being a notable example in which enthusiasm for their use ran to excess.

The supplementary and related use of objectives for evaluation criteria is widespread in both internal and external examinations and on school report proformas[14] as well as in research studies. As a part of the I.E.A. study of science achievement,[15] increased insight into the purposes of school science practical work was gained through the development of a taxonomy of practical abilities as a result of having to create practical work test items which would be applicable in diverse contexts, and this is an illustration of how the obligation to evaluate the curriculum assists in the definition of its purposes. Although, under Stenhouse's influence,* the Schools Council Humanities Curriculum Project did not develop a list of objectives, 10 criteria whereby the quality of students' work is to be judged were given[16] which are, in fact, close to generalized (cf. specific) behavioural goals. The work executed by the Farmington Trust in the late 1960s on moral education is a further interesting example in which analysis of the kinds of behaviour which a morally educated person might be expected to display gave rise to the following criteria which implicitly provide generalized objectives for moral education programmes as well as indices for their evaluation.[18]

Skills of the morally educated person
1 Able to treat other people as equals.
2 Having awareness of the feelings, wants and interests of the self and others.
3 Knowing facts relevant to moral decisions and personal relationships.
4 Able to formulate rules and make rational decisions relating to other peoples' interests.
5 As 4, but relating to self interest.
6 Able to put formulated moral rules into practice.

---

*Stenhouse has been the most ardent British critic of curriculum models enshrining 'objectives'. However, he has taken the term in its most frequent 'classical' usage in the U.S.A. as 'prespecifications of terminal student behaviours' to which most British writers, including Kerr and Hirst, do not conform. Stenhouse does not, it seems, object to educational intentions or aims but to a particular way of stating all or most intentions in advance,[17] which clearly would deny the unpredictability of many learning situations in which sensitive teachers not only modify on the spot the learning experiences provided, but at least some of their short-term objectives. While Stenhouse is properly concerned with the dynamics of teaching as process, some of his implicit criticism of British authors on the topic of objectives are wide of the mark, being based upon a misunderstanding about terminology.

Through the assessment of these criteria using simulated concrete examples, such as car driving behaviour, individuals or groups may be given, in principle at least, a moral education rating.

Hence the literature shows that objectives have helped in a wide variety of disciplines, topics and areas for training.

CONCLUDING COMMENTS

So much has been written in recent years on the topic of educational objectives that it seems reasonable to conclude both that the topic is an important one within curriculum design and that there can be little which is novel to add to the literature in this domain! Despite the controversies in the literature, which frequently originate from the bipoles of viewing curriculum either as 'science' or as 'art and craft', educational aims, intentions, goals, objectives are professional necessities rather than luxuries for the philosophically inclined. Despite some evidence[19] that both primary and secondary schoolteachers find their use difficult and concentrate most of their professional efforts elsewhere, there is a wealth of other indications that curriculum developers (including local teachers' groups), evaluators and examiners cannot manage without them. Some of the controversies about teaching methods and strategies could be more enlightened if the underlying differences of value and aim were drawn out.[20]

To most, educational objectives are thus a help and not a hindrance, though we need to be aware of their dangers, which are referred to in the more recent manuals.[21] Davies puts it well when he writes in his preface:[22]

Objectives, fortunately, are not a universal remedy or panacea for all the ills facing education today. They are simply a useful tool or guide, neither more nor less, which is more helpful in some situations than in others. The issue is one of appropriateness, not only in terms of their usage, but also in terms of the amount of specificity required in their definition. Richness in teaching and learning need not be sacrificed for the sake of clarity, nor need romance be sacrificed for the sake of precision . . . As John Dewey has pointed out, 'acting with an aim is one with acting intelligently'. So it is with objectives. Thinking intelligently about objectives, however, is as important as acting intelligently with them. Knowing about objectives is essential, but it is not enough. They can be as trite, ordinary and limiting as you like to make them. What is required is a 'new think'. This involves putting objectives into perspective, and then handling them in a sensitive and creative manner. They should be viewed as a resource for teaching and learning, rather than as a set of blinkers or restrainers.

Nevertheless we need to recognize that in curriculum reform we have strayed markedly from the logical, relevant, if a little simplistic approach of the founding father of curriculum objectives, Franklin Bobbitt. In 1924 he suggested[23] that in building a school curriculum one should take as the theoretical point of departure an analysis of the contents of adults' working and domestic lives; an education which claims to be true to life and wishes to prepare persons for the later demands made upon them needs, he argued, to be tuned into those specific performances in the varied social contexts of their application.

In the more dynamic and changing society in which we now live it would be difficult to apply Bobbitt's principle, but, with widespread unemployment, particularly among young people, staring us in the face as we enter the 1980s, and in the light of the widespread disintegration of family life[24] upon which successful schooling depends so crucially, we cannot deny at least some of its appeal for the contemporary world. With the apparently all too slow response of the formal curriculum to rapidly changing factors in the external world, a far more radical approach may be necessary. That may be quite another story, but if radical curricular reform begins it will find an analysis of its objectives unavoidable if its character is to be widely understood, shared and implemented.

1. B. S. Bloom *et al.*, *Taxonomy of Educational Objectives*, Handbooks I and II (1956 and 1964).
2. I. K. Davies, *Objectives in Curriculum Design* (1976).
3. L. Stenhouse, *An Introduction to Curriculum Research and Development* (1975).
4. P. H. Hirst, 'What is teaching?', in *Journal of Curriculum Studies*, III (I) (1971), 5–18.
5. Davies, *op. cit.*; Stenhouse, *op. cit.*; see also E. W. Jenkins and R. C. Whitfield (eds), *Readings in Science Education* (1974).
6. R. C. Whitfield, *Disciplines of the Curriculum* (1971), and ch. 2 of M. Holt (ed.), *The 16-19 Curriculum* (1980).
7 P. H. Hirst, *Knowledge and Schooling* (1974).
8 P. H. Phenix, *Realms of Meaning* (1964).
9 R. L. Derr, *A Taxonomy of the Social Purposes of Public Schools* (New York, 1973).
10. R. C. Whitfield, *Curriculum Planning, Teaching and Educational Accountability*, Aston Educational Enquiry Monograph 6 (reprinted 1978).
11. R C. Whitfield, 'Curriculum objectives, examinations and curriculum change', in *Cambridge Journal of Education*, II (II) (1972), 76–91.
12. *Ibid.*

13. Schools Council/Nuffield Foundation, *With Objectives in Mind* (1972).
14. See for example Scottish Council for Research in Education, *Pupils in Profile* (1977).
15. L. C. Comber and J. P. Keeves, *Science Education in Nineteen Countries* (1973). (Unpublished taxonomy of practical abilities developed by J. F. Eggleston and R. C. Whitfield, 1968.)
16. Schools Council/Nuffield Foundation, *The Humanities Project: An introduction* (1970), 33–6.
17. L. Stenhouse, letter to editor of *Cambridge Journal of Education*, III (II) (1973), 116, and *Paedagogica Europaea*, VI (1970), 73–83.
18. J. Wilson, B. Sugarman and N. Williams, *An Introduction to Moral Education* (1967), and J. Wilson, *Moral Education and the Curriculum* (1970).
19. P. H. Taylor (ed.), *Aims, Influence and Change in the Primary School Curriculum*, N.F.E.R. (1975), and *idem, How Teachers Plan their Courses*, N.F.E.R. (1970).
20. See for example unit AIM 1 of *Activities and Experiences* (1974).
21. N. E. Gronlund, *Stating Behavioural Objectives for Classroom Instruction* (1978); Davies, *op. cit.*
22. *Ibid.*
23. F. Bobbitt, *How to Make a Curriculum* (Boston, 1924).
24. R. C. Whitfield, *Educating for Family Responsibility*, in report of October 1978 conference on Family Life, National Children's Home (1979), and *Education for Family Life: Towards preventive policies for child care* (1980).

3 The selection of curriculum content: issues and problems

DAVID TOMLEY

Why we teach what we teach is an extremely complex issue which cannot be separated from a consideration of the history, social context and the values of past and present society. In the case of science the problem is even more pressing because of what is called 'the knowledge explosion'. Over a decade ago it was estimated that in terms of hard facts, knowledge of science and technology was doubling within a 10-year period.[1] This exponential growth shows no sign of reaching a plateau. Science therefore poses many of the problems involved in the selection of curriculum content in their most pressing form. In particular, problems centring around the teaching of biology and the related sciences have multiplied in a most spectacular fashion so that according to one commentator,[2] 'While chemistry was perhaps the science of the 1920's and physics that of the 1940's and 1950's, I am convinced that biology will be the fashionable science of the 1970's and 1980's.'

In examining some of the issues concerning the selection of content it seems appropriate to make a case study of recent developments in biological education where, because of its recent rapid growth rate, the decisions are more pressing but very similar to those in other areas. It took nearly 50 years from the discovery of x-rays to their inclusion as a topic in most A-level physics syllabuses. Simple treatment of D.N.A. and the double helix arrived inside five years. A problem facing the 'amateur historian' in seeking explanation for such changes in curriculum content is the lack of documentation relating to the deliberations of either the subject panels of Examination Boards or of the curriculum development teams. Nevertheless, an examination of the end products, be it the revised syllabus or the new curriculum package, would suggest that certain factors exerted a disproportionate influence on the decision-making process. In this case study I shall trace these influences as seen in the most recent developments in biology teaching and argue that a different kind of balance needs to be struck if we are to come to terms with the knowledge explosion in any future attempts at curriculum renewal.

THE CONTENT OF BIOLOGY COURSES 1900–50

To reach any kind of understanding of the present position it is necessary to look back at earlier developments. Up to the mid-1950s the biology taught in universities had changed little from the start of the century. Parker and Haswell, B.E.P.S., Strasburger and Smith were names known to generations of students. This was reflected at school level where texts like Grove and Newell's *Animal Biology*, Lowson's *Botany* and Maud Jepson's *Biological Drawings* could be issued without fail year after year.[3] Fingers of generations of sixth-form school biology students became pickled and their mucous membranes damaged by the formalin that bathed and preserved the dogfish, frogs and rats which were hacked to bits week after week, as the 'types', respresentative of different groups, were checked off the syllabus. The teachers were keen and enthusiastic about their subject and sought to keep up-to-date with new developments and add to their already overloaded teaching schemes still more information. A teacher-dominated approach was essential; there was so much to cover. The emphasis was on content, transmitted to the pupils' notebooks from the teacher's, often by dictation and sometimes, it seemed, without passing through the brain of either! The transmission model of teaching was universal. Essentially it was a case of 'I know, you don't; sit still and listen and I'll tell you'. But at least when it came to the examinations the pupil and the teacher were on the same side – both against the examiner. The skill of question spotting was finely honed. As the envelope containing the exam papers was deftly slit open the pupil could tell from the teacher's face or even by his thumbs-up sign that this year's bankers had come up!

The university-controlled examination boards produced the same form of examination papers year after year. Crossland[4] in an analysis of School Certificates and O-level biology papers from four boards between 1948 and 1962 found 80 per cent of questions devoted to the acquisition of facts, about 5 per cent to application and interpretation of data and about 15 per cent to designing and planning experiments.

School science, then, was strongly subject-focussed and content-orientated. There were strict rules about what constituted science and scientific behaviour. A high premium was placed on academic scholarship involving a deep and systematic concern for the content of the subject. Thus science reflected the history of the subject and of the people teaching it. It was a socializing of the young into the traditions, thoughts and behaviour patterns of their elders. There was a clear hierarchical, almost linear relationship between pupil, teacher and university tutor. Schoolmasters were scientists first and teachers second.

Good descriptions of pre-war grammar-school science are to be found in the writings of C. P. Snow and William Cooper. Yet Cooper's hero in

The Struggle of Albert Woods offers an alternative view of science in his description of the process of discovery. For the scientist this 'leap in the dark' needs to be viewed in the same way as creating a work of art is for an artist or writing a poem is for a poet. Scientists can be seen as human and fallible, subject to the same feelings and pressures as other people. Their work may be viewed as creative and imaginative and not necessarily dull and routine.

None of this seems to have filtered into the teaching of science in school. For pupils involved in Pritchard's 1935 study, chemistry was 'just a mass of facts and the equations and calculations were hard to understand'.[5] Science was represented as a known corpus of knowledge and scientific method seen as a dry, never-failing approach to solving problems. Practical work was mostly verification and always written up in the passive voice thereby eliminating any sense of the excitement which the pupil might have felt at his involvement in the discovery process. The truer picture of the frustrations and blind alleys experienced by all scientists followed by those periods of elation when the problem was solved thus never emerged.[6]

The decade after the end of the Second World War brought an increasing awareness of the importance of science and technology in our society and a corresponding concern that little was being done to improve the output or quality of scientists. Numerous interacting effects including the Cold War, anxieties over defence, the persisting shadow of the Second World War, the economic and manpower positions, all helped to heighten the awareness in political and scientific circles of the need to develop technological and technical education and to sharpen up what was being taught as science. University departments expanded and entry requirements grew harder as more young people opted to read science subjects. Acceptance at university at that time did not mean an automatic grant from the state. Grants were awarded on a county basis – county scholarships – and some counties were richer and some more generous than others. So the students worked. There was no time to question. More scientists were needed and this included science teachers who, about this time, were excused from national service if they had a good honours degree.

This growth in demand for a technically-educated workforce meant that some science had to be taught to all secondary pupils. In theory, secondary modern schools, set up after the 1944 Education Act, gave science teachers freedom from the strait-jacket of examinations, since external examinations were not allowed in these establishments. The pupils worked on projects of their own choosing, and could, if they wished, concentrate on aspects of applied science more suited to the sorts of jobs they would be doing when they left school. Within a few short years of their existence, however, pressure from parents and teachers meant that most of these schools, too, were following similar, if watered down, courses to those of the grammar schools.

Hargreaves[7] suggests that teachers have always been concerned with their status even as far back as the nineteenth century when school inspectors and public school teachers were typically Oxbridge men, while the elementary school teachers were college trained and of lower class backgrounds. Even with the change-over to a comprehensive system this schism remains, placing teachers within either the *grammar-public* tradition or the *elementary-secondary modern* one. Status is closely linked to expertise in teaching; professional status therefore rests on having 'esoteric' knowledge. This may often be a mixture of the practical and the theoretical, but it is part of the professional's claim that such practice should rest upon some branch of knowledge to which practioners are privy by virtue of their long study under masters who are already members of the profession. The 'esoteric' knowledge and expertise of the *grammar-public* tradition of teachers is their specialist knowledge of their subject, validated by the possession of an appropriate university degree.

Science teachers of the *grammar-public* tradition are to a large extent mirror images of scientists in universities. Their 'esoteric' knowledge is theoretical rather than practical and this is reflected in the type of curriculum they teach. Teachers of the *elementary-secondary modern* tradition, with less subject knowledge and weaker subject identity, have less in common with the 'pure' scientists. They therefore tend to give more emphasis to pedagogical skills, the needs of pupils and theories of mental development when justifying the appropriateness of course content.

Since the 1960s this schism between teachers has become even more pronounced. The B.Ed. degree has offered a new form of 'esoteric' knowledge: that of the social sciences. For those teaching pre-adolescents, this new degree has legitimated their professional status. Sadly for college-trained teachers working with pupils over 14 years old, Piaget stopped at 13, so there is no adolescent equivalent of 'esoteric' knowledge from the social sciences for them! The B.Ed. has been no substitute for the B.Sc. and in practice subject expertise rather than pedagogical knowledge has therefore continued to be the main criterion for judging the effectiveness of the science teacher.

CHANGES FROM THE MID-1950s – A PERIOD OF CURRICULUM RENEWAL

The 1950s and early 1960s were a time of considerable expansion in biological understanding and knowledge. Watson and Crick were unravelling the structure and function of D.N.A., Pauling was working on proteins and Tinbergen and Lorenz were advancing our understanding of animal behaviour. Studies in molecular biology, viral and bacterial genetics and microbiology took off. Systematics, anatomy and morphology were taking a back seat. Letters in *Nature* from eminent zoologists and botanists questioned the validity of the separate disciplines of botany and zoology as so many of the new fields used methods, techniques and material from whichever discipline seemed appropriate.[8] The nature of biology was changing.

In 1958 the Trustees of the Gulbenkian Foundation offered to provide the University of Birmingham with money to enquire into an educational topic of urgent current interest. The University's association with the Northern Universities Joint Matriculation Board resulted in an enquiry into the Advanced-level syllabuses in Science offered by that Board. This represented the first funded curriculum movement in this country. The Biology Panel consisted of seven university members and five teachers (though six were invited). The teachers were selected after consultation with local branches of the Teachers' Association. Given the context of the Advanced-level examination, all the teachers had to have a high degree of subject specialism and, coming as they did from grammar, direct grant and independent schools, were strongly in the *grammar-public* tradition.

The Panel's report[9] included the recommendations that the A-level botany and zoology examinations should be discontinued, that a new A-level in biology should replace the existing one and that schools be encouraged to teach biology in the sixth form. They considered in some detail the form that both the theory and practical examinations should take and went on to discuss the proposed content of a new A-level biology syllabus. In this context it is of interest to note that the Panel believed the course,

> should be one which stresses the underlying principles of biology, and which shows not only the fundamental differences between plant and animal, but above all, the fundamental similarities of living things, and which pays due attention (and no more) to the various natural biological divisions, one of which is that between plant and animal.

No species other than man was named in their proposed examination syllabus. Notes to the syllabus were provided in order: to expand and explain items which, in the Panel's view, required it; to separate related aspects which were often confused, and to indicate the areas which 'are now regarded as being of general importance but which are not yet treated adequately in the usual text-books, e.g. Nucleic acid'. Here was a proposal to include in an A-level syllabus the chemical structure of D.N.A. when it was still hypothetical and only five years after its structure had been proposed by Watson and Crick. The relationship between genes and enzymes was also included, as was something on the genetic code.

A little earlier a working party of the Science Masters' Association had produced a new Policy Statement concerned with science teaching in grammar schools.[10] It recommended a pruning of the A-level science syllabus, that all sixth-form pupils should follow a cultural course in science and that all pupils should have the same amount of time for science up to the end of their fifth year. It made the point in the introduction that 'schools ... have the duty of presenting science as part of our common cultural and humanistic heritage'. The aims of science teaching were expressed as follows:[11]

1 To lead pupils to observe, and to solve problems by controlled experiments, to draw conclusions from observations, and to appreciate the systematic laws and principles of science,
2 To give knowledge and understanding of the origin and development of science, of the achievements of scientific pioneers and of the implications, now and in the future, of modern scientific and technological development,
3 For science specialists, to provide a suitable preparation for further scientific or technological education.

As a result of distributing some 14,000 copies of this policy statement to members of the S.M.A. and Association for Women Science Teachers (A.W.S.T.) to industry, learned societies, the educational press, the Ministry, and local education committees, they were encouraged by the response to pursue the matter further.

The result in 1961 was a joint statement by the S.M.A. and A.W.S.T., containing detailed sections on what sort of biology, chemistry and physics should be taught in grammar schools both below, and in, the sixth form. It also focussed on *how* science should be taught. The subject panels attempted to produce a teaching scheme with notes expanding various sections, but found this unrealistic and realized that something much bigger, needing proper financial backing was required. A chance remark, by two members of the S.M.A. involved in the syllabus revision exercise, to a past president of the Association, Sir Alexander Todd (later Lord Todd), led to his suggesting that they approach the Nuffield Foundation for support.[12]

The Foundation asked for a detailed statement of the needs and of how the Associations proposed to meet these. The Associations' submission went to the meeting of the Nuffield Foundation Trustees in December 1961. As it happened, the Director of the Nuffield Foundation, Dr Leslie Farrer-Brown, was interested in bringing about change in school science. He had been talking to John Lewis, a physics teacher from Malvern College, who had recently returned from a visit to Russia where he had been impressed with the centrally-produced resources that the teachers there had to use. It struck Farrer-Brown that while central direction was unacceptable here, the production of top-quality materials would be invaluable as resources for science teachers to use.[13] The Director himself submitted two papers to the Trustees' meeting, one outlining the need for educative research and experiment and the other on the teaching of science and mathematics.

As a result of that meeting and one further meeting the Trustees agreed to support a curriculum development project in science. Discussion with officials from the Ministry of Education ensued and it was agreed to concentrate initially on O-level courses. Informal discussion took place with several industries having an interest in science education and likely to provide help and experience. The S.M.A./A.W.S.T. were kept aware of progress and in April 1962 Sir David Eccles, the Minister of Education, in reply to a parliamentary question announced the setting up of the Nuffield Foundation Science Teaching Project.[14]

Consideration of school science had also been taking place in the United States. Undoubtedly their curriculum developments in physics, chemistry and biology influenced the British ones. The American nationally-funded development projects all received a further injection of funds when Sputnik 1, the first Russian satellite, was launched in October 1957. But that incident was not, as it is sometimes said to have been, the trigger for the American developments. Each American project was headed by an eminent university scientist and except in the case of biology most of the writers of material were from universities and colleges too.[15] The projects were developed by a central team of writers, seconded from their existing work, and backing the writing team was a consultative committee of eminent scientists. The whole venture was subject or discipline-based, reflecting the strong position of the subject lobby at that time and the faith that people had in the centrality of the discipline. The Biological Sciences Curriculum Study (B.S.C.S.) produced three versions of the same course based on different levels of organization: the *subcellular*, the *organism* and the *population*.

In Britain, the consultative committee of the Nuffield Science Teaching Project, after an initial flirtation with the idea of having an eminent scientist as organizer of each project, came round to the idea that they should be designed by teachers for teachers. Certainly this was the case with the Nuffield O-level Biology Project and later with the Nuffield A-level Biology Project. The development teams contained nobody who had not been a teacher and the majority were still practising teachers, albeit that most of them were from independent or direct grant schools. The aims of these courses make splendid reading,[16] and, in my view, the people who developed them should take considerable satisfaction from the achievement. Yet despite the extent of teacher participation, the British courses do not differ radically from their American counterparts.

The content, to embody the aims of the Nuffield Courses, was decided by the teams after a wide consultation with universities and professional bodies, due consideration of the Scottish development at the time,[17] the Association of Science Education policy statements and the best practice known to the developers and their contacts. The Nuffield science schemes were the most important curriculum developments to have taken place in this country. They aimed at producing a radical reform of school science. They were a response to political, social, economic and educational pressures and in part a product of individual initiative and action.[18] Like the American developments they were discipline-centred curriculum developments, the evolutionary outcome of many years' work by small groups working through the S.M.A. and A.W.S.T. They showed a belief in the subject disciplines and were a reflection of the pervading values of the time and of the power of the subject associations, professional institutes and university departments.

Despite attempts to marry the content and the pedagogy and so bridge the gap between the two teaching traditions and to include applied aspects of the subject, the courses had a very academic bias. Given the background of the course teams, the strength of the subject lobby at that time and the audience for whom the courses were intended, such an outcome was perhaps inevitable. And once the new curriculum materials passed into the hands of teachers outside the immediate influence of the development team, pedagogic objectives were forgotten.

The central tenet of the Nuffield O-level biology course was pupil-centred enquiry and yet when science teachers were observed, using Science Teaching Observation Schedule (STOS),[19] the majority of biology teachers were found to teach didactically so that many of the higher aims of the Nuffield course were not translated into practice.[20] In the face of such evidence it might be argued that this curriculum development failed.

The Nuffield projects, however, can claim three considerable successes. First, marked change has resulted because of them. Nearly 20 per cent of candidates taking O-level science examinations take Nuffield science examinations. New textbooks and revision of old ones have drawn heavily on 'Nuffield' ideas, as have revised examination syllabuses of most examination boards.[21] Second, the influence of the project has extended to all levels and stages of secondary schooling. Many C.S.E. Mode III courses are modelled on Nuffield courses, so that teaching can be organized in wide ability groups, thereby delaying the time when a choice has to be made about which external examination a pupil is entered for. Third, the courses provided excellent resources from which the majority of science teachers have benefited. Only the biology course provided pupils' texts and the development team did not anticipate such a rigid approach being adopted in the use of these.[22] They certainly did not expect a second edition!

The project team aimed to provide, and I believe did provide 'a contemporary course designed to foster a critical approach to the subject with an emphasis on experimentation and enquiry rather than on mere factual assimilation.'[23] However, as Kerr pointed out, 'Commonly, curriculum discussion in schools, colleges and universities is about the *content* [my italics] of syllabuses',[24] and although the Nuffield biology team clearly recognized this and strove to direct the teachers' attention to the wider implications of teaching science, arguing that 'The development of a more contemporary, experimental and enquiring attitude in teaching is going to demand consideration not so much of *what* is taught (although this is obviously important) as of *how* the teaching is carried out',[25] the preoccupation of the schools with the content of the course remained, for as Grace Monger in her follow-up enquiry some years later reported, 'It is clear from the comments on the questionnaire that teachers are occupied with the *content* of the texts rather than with the *teaching method* and approach.'[26] So even though the developers tried to make use of the new subject matter to engineer changes in teaching style, at the end of the day the debate never got beyond discussion of the merits of the course content.

TOWARDS A NEW APPROACH TO CURRICULUM BUILDING

Given the strength of the traditions that have been described and the lack of adequate theory to underpin the pedagogical alternative, it might be said, with hindsight, that no other outcome was possible. As Becher and Maclure argue,[27]

Academic subjects enjoy a socio-political entity in their own right. They represent powerful interest groups, legitimated and given sanction not only by the qualifications they award but also by the fact that publishers' lists and library catalogues faithfully reflect the categories which they impose. The secondary curriculum can be seen as a territory, carved up and balkanised into a series of separate empires, over which the more powerful disciplines hold sway. Operating mainly from a series of bases within higher education they seek to colonize and inculcate the secondary schools with their values and their forms of thought.

This well illustrates the strength and hold that a subject-centred curriculum has on our secondary schools and though it could be argued, as perhaps Hirst would argue, that as the disciplines embody distinct forms of knowledge, each with different conceptual structure, methods of enquiry and tests for truth,[28] it is pertinent to ask whether the subject-based curriculum is now the most appropriate for schools of the future.

Kerr, in the introduction to *Changing the Curriculum*, suggests, 'It may be that some new subjects or combinations of related disciplines should replace part of the conventional material, so that the structure of the total field of knowledge and the range of experience provided would be more comprehensive and relevant', and in his inaugural lecture makes the same point more strongly: 'An unfortunate result of contemporary curriculum developments, even in the junior schools, has been to focus attention on individual disciplines without concern for their relationships to other fields and to neglect the overall structure of the whole school programme.'[29] He goes on to urge a re-examination of the disciplines as sources for learning,

> The selection of characteristic principles and concepts in any particular discipline is too big a job for one person. It is a task for a team which should include university specialists and other consultants as well as teachers. . . Having designed a new course, the team of teachers and specialists should keep it under review.[30]

With the prevailing attitudes and values of the 1960s it is probably naive to have expected greater change to have occurred as a consequence of the curriculum development that took place then. But a wider view must be taken now. In today's schools a teacher is no longer just a subject specialist; his role is much wider, reflecting the fact that society has altered too. Yet, in the next wave of reform we seem bent on repeating the mistakes of the past.

The influence of the disciplines and the *grammar-public* tradition of teachers can clearly be seen in the composition of the commissioned group based on the Institute of Biology which was asked by the Schools Council to design syllabuses for N- and F-level biology. In the introduction to their report it is claimed that, 'The Institute is well placed to draw on the views of biologists with a wide spectrum of experience and opinion about the teaching and the examining of biology at the sixth form level and to form a group which represented this spectrum of opinion.'[31] The group consisted of two people from polytechnics, one person from a university, one person (the Education Officer) from the Institute of Biology who also acted as secretary, two people from independent schools, one from a grammar school and only two from comprehensive schools. If the corresponding members of the group were included it adds four more from universities, two of whom were from education faculties. Setting aside the points that could be made about the sex ratio and the fact that both comprehensive representatives were female, it is highly doubtful that the Institute had formed a group representative of the opinion about teaching biology to the target population at which particularly the N-level examination was to be aimed.

What the group does represent is the power structure. For similar reasons, when G.C.E. examination boards boast of the numbers of teachers on their subject panels in science it is not really very inform- ative. The majority of science teachers are of the **grammar-public** tradition with values similar to the representatives from universities and in such situations; in any case, teachers may often retreat and become defensive before the remarks made by specialists from university subject departments.

The latest A.S.E. consultative document, Alternatives for Science Education,[32] outlines many of the changes which schools have recently undergone. The move to comprehensive education with its underlying ideological and educational implications, the liberalization of the pri- mary school curriculum following the ending of the 11+, has meant access for all to a common school and a common culture. Teachers have now to consider the appropriateness of what they do at all levels. Although amalgamation of grammar with secondary modern schools once again revealed the schism of the two traditions within the teaching profession, the development of C.S.E. Mode III courses, schemes for mixed-ability teaching, individualized learning and worksheets have forced some reappraisal on both sides. This, however, has taken up hours of the teachers' time both in meetings and in preparation of new materials.

The development of faculty systems and pastoral structures has also put extra pressure on the teachers and widened their roles. A biology teacher, for example, could have a group of 15 students in the sixth year going on to A-level, some of whom would be taking physics and chemistry, but most of whom may well be taking subjects like geog- raphy, English or music. So the teacher's work has become harder, now that most of the group have less science in their background. In addition he could be taking wide ability groups in the fourth and fifth year, some of whom would ultimately take G.C.E. O-level, others a Mode III C.S.E. examination, developed so that it could be taught alongside the O-level course, and still others no examination at all. Again the hetero- geneity of the group has made the teacher's work more difficult. The same teacher may teach environmental science and social biology and be developing, with other staff from other faculties, courses in health education, human physiology and child care. Wearing a different hat the same teacher may also be a year head in the pastoral system of the school with five or six tutor groups to co-ordinate, reports to organize, parents to see and behaviour to check. These sorts of role are not atypical and of course the demands on the teacher's time do not end there. There would still be the staff meetings, faculty meetings, in-service education meetings that would need attending and preparing for, and possibly even the chess club to organize!

With this sort of workload it is no wonder that yesterday's innovative courses become the established courses of today. The Nuffield Foundation received requests to revise and reprint their O-level biology course. Examination boards are asked for more and more guidance on exactly what to teach, what practicals to use, what books to buy. The J.M.B., I know, resists these requests as it does not wish there to become a J.M.B. prescribed and approved list of practicals and books for its biology syllabuses. But it is understandable, with the changes of the last decade in schools, why the teachers ask for this help. They simply have no time.

At the same time, British society has been developing an increasingly egalitarian outlook; there has been erosion of traditional authority, cherished values and standards and attempts to redefine its basis. Society now is pluralistic, its values are varied and negotiated. There is a crisis of confidence in our education system, a realization that education itself does not bring about social change. There is a demand for a greater accountability; for others apart from teachers to have a say about what goes on in schools. Schools serve society and are therefore accountable to that society. If the freedom which teachers value is to be maintained then they have a responsibility to involve others in the debate about any reappraisal of the content of the curriculum.

What should emerge from the previous discussion is that the issues of the selection of objectives, given that the term is not restricted to a narrow definition in terms of behavioural outcomes, and the selection of content are inextricably linked together. As Kerr argued over a decade ago, 'The objectives should be identified first, as we cannot, or should not, decide "what" or "how" to teach in any situation until we know "why" we are doing it.'[33] For Kerr the needs of the pupils and the influence of society as well as the underlying structure of the respective disciplines each had its contribution to make in defining these objectives. Kerr no doubt underestimated the strength of the traditional science lobby, the emphasis on the teaching of science rather than the teaching of teaching in so many of the Post Graduate Certificate Courses and the strong historical links between the grammar and public schools and the professional science teaching associations. Those responsible for developing Nuffield science schemes began with the best of intentions but they would have needed to be both psychologists and sociologists to have overcome these historical antecedents.

Future curriculum renewal will have to begin by examining the needs of its major client, the pupil in the schools. While Hirst's acknowledgment that 'Decision about the content of courses cannot be taken without careful regard to the abilities and interests of the students for whom they are designed',[34] has gradually taken on more substance in the wake of problems connected with the move to comprehensive schools, mixed-ability teaching and the like, there is still precious little known about how learning takes place or about the development stages through which adolescents pass or about the role of language in learning. Although the work of Barnes,[35] Britton,[36] Martin,[37] Shayer[38] and Sutton[39] has begun to redress this imbalance there is still considerable research to be undertaken before the needs of pupils can be incorporated into the design and planning of curriculum development on any systematic basis. In the absence of this research evidence it must surely be correct to give more weight than is currently allowed to the opinions of the teachers who are engaged in instructing the target population and might therefore be expected to know more about them than do the keepers of the discipline.

The relationship between science and society, the third source of Kerr's objectives, is also changing rapidly. More and more segments of the population are demanding a say in the school curriculum. Science sits on a much lower pedestal than it did during the 1960s. Few think that science *per se* can solve society's problems and among those who do not understand the methodology there is a strong distrust of both science and scientists.

Perhaps most important therefore is the need to demystify the process of scientific enquiry and eliminate the contempt often shown for the potential contribution of applied science and technology in solving society's ills. Science teachers are among the worst offenders in this regard and there are many who still believe that industry and the world of work are still something slightly sordid to which only the less able pupils should be condemned. Undoubtedly, this ethos stems in part from the *grammar-public* school tradition of science teaching with its strong links with the pure science faculties of the universities where, as Kelly[40] says, 'Pure research has the respectable prestige of the university backed up by the publication and academic honours system. Applied research is "tainted" by the profit motive of industry.'

The whole school system often appears to support and approve the elevation of pure over applied science. At one famous public school only pure scientists are excused prayers, on the grounds not of potential atheism, but because of the time needed to set up equipment. Many of the other grammar and public schools built their science laboratories as an afterthought yet it is still often the practice in the newest comprehensive school to put the science laboratories in a separate wing of their own. No doubt practical consideration of safety and ease of delivering equipment are sufficient architectural reasons but the consequence of all this is to remove both the scientists and science from the mainstream of school life. All too often the teachers take their break-time separated from the main staffroom, drink their coffee in the prep room where, as part of the general conversation, they can decide their attitude to current school issues. They have a strong sense of corporate identity which sets them apart from their colleagues.

SOME CURRENT QUESTIONS AND OPINIONS

If school science is to become more responsive to the needs of pupils and to society then changes in the existing methods of curriculum development will be necessary. Attempts at integrating science with other areas by grafting social issues onto the discipline[41] do not really seem to be the answer. If science itself is to become more acceptable to a larger school population as a subject of study then what scientists do and how they do it will have to be seen as a human and creative activity in its own right. Lord Bullock in his Presidential address to the A.S.E. urged a similar change of attitude:

> the more it is possible, legitimately, to move away from a mono-
> lithic, mechanistic, dehumanised image of science; to establish a
> view of it as a humane study, deeply concerned both with man and
> society; providing scope for imagination and compassion as well as
> observation and analysis; and calling, in those who succeed in it, for
> outstanding personal qualities, the easier it will be to overcome the
> sense of alienation which turns many young people away from
> it.[42]

In the context of biology Peter Kelly[43] has suggested that while the values that science offers should not be undermined, the description of the process could be made more realistic. He argues for making uncommon knowledge more common, and in the context of biological education including what he calls 'issue studies' as well as 'knowledge studies'. The former type of study links biology with the reality of peoples' lives involving groups with different viewpoints, raising moral questions and often having no right answers to issues raised. But such studies cannot be embarked on without some knowledge so that a balance is needed. Kelly also advocates a 'biosocial dimension', one which has roots in the physical make-up of an organism but which is expressed in a social context, as part of school biological education. A study of it would 'bring biology, particularly human biology, into liaison with aspects of sociology, psychology, and anthropology so that by introducing this biosocial dimension within biological education we add to its wealth of perspective and enquiry'. Pupils will therefore 'learn something more of the many ways we have to look at life'.

Kelly concludes by saying that: 'as a component of general education, biological education in its broader and better sense, should intimately mesh the strands of scientific knowledge, a person's individual and community needs, and a consideration of moral values, into a firm educational fabric.'[44] While pointing the way forward there are still some formidable problems to be solved before Kelly's ideas can be translated into a practical curriculum. First and foremost is the question of the balance to be struck between the different areas of content and here Monger's[45] enquiry into the working of the O-level Nuffield biology course suggests that some of the necessary changes will involve:

1 More emphasis on the biosocial areas of the subject;
2 More on the technological aspects of the subject;
3 A need to consider the role of chemistry, physics and mathematics in relation to biological science;
4 A need to consider areas of social implications and practical application.

Additional features which teachers may wish to include in future revisions centre around attempts to relate existing topics to applied biology and to link them to more modern developments; issues which have received very little attention in the past.

Currently the specialist subject association has taken up this debate.[46] In the light of previous experience, however, it would seem that the issues raised are now too big to be left solely to one group, especially one which still maintains its strong links with the subject specialism of the past. Perhaps what is needed are 'better ways of reaching a collective view about curricular priorities which could then provide a framework within which creative developments might take place.'[47] What is certain is that if the new wave of curriculum development is to overcome the weaknesses of the earlier schemes a far wider participation of a broad spectrum of the teaching profession will be an essential pre-requisite.

1. D. J. Price, *Little Science, Big Science* (New York, 1963).
2. Alexander King, O.E.C.D. Seminar on *Reform in Biology Teaching* (1962).
3. Based on F. E. G. Cox, 'Changing trends in biological syllabuses', in University of London, *University Entrance and School Examinations Council Conference*, Report No.15 (1975).
4. R. W. Crossland, *The Outcomes of Science Teaching: Address to the Science Masters' Association*, mimeographed (Jan. 1963).
5. R. A. Pritchard, 'The relative popularity of secondary school subjects at various ages', in *British Journal of Educational Psychology*, v (1935), 157–79, 229–41.
6. J. F. Brierley, 'Science for the arts specialist', in *Schools Council Working Paper No. 4. Science in the Sixth Form* (1966); Mary Waring, *Social Pressures and Curriculum Innovation, A study of the Nuffield Foundation Science Teaching Project* (1979).

7. D. Hargreaves, 'What teaching does to teachers and what teachers can do about it', in *PRISE News*, ed. Robin Chambers (Spring 1979).
8. See for example letters by H. V. Wyatt, *Nature*, CXCI (1961), 960–1; H. E. Street, *Nature*, CXCII (1961), 416–7; D. G. Catcheside, *Nature*, CXCVII (1963), 427; W. B. Yapp, *Nature*, CXCXIII (1963), 409.
9. Gulbenkian Enquiry, *Report of an Enquiry into the Suitability of the General Certificate of Education Advanced Level Syllabuses in Science as a Preparation for Direct Entry into First Degree Courses in the Faculty of Science*, Report of the Biology Panel (1959).
10. Science Masters' Association, *Science and Education: A policy statement by the Committee of the Science Masters' Association* (1957).
11. *Ibid.*
12. M. R. H. Waring, 'Aspects of the dynamics of curriculum reform in secondary school science', (unpublished Ph.D. thesis, Centre for Science Education, University of London, 1975).
13. *Ibid.*
14. *Ibid.*
15. P. J. Kelly, 'Curriculum development and the curriculum mechanism: an account of the Nuffield 'A' level biology project in relation to the concept of the curriculum mechanism' (unpublished Ph.D. thesis, University of London, 1971).
16. Nuffield Foundation, *Nuffield Foundation Science Teaching Project: A level biology, aims and outline scheme* (1965); *idem*, *Nuffield Foundation Science Teaching Project: Synopsis of the Nuffield biology course ('O' level)* (1966).
17. Scottish Education Department, *Science in Secondary Schools* (1951).
18. Kelly, *op. cit.*
19. J. F. Eggleston, M. J. Galton and M. E. Jones, *A Science Teaching Observation Schedule*, Schools Council Research Series (1975).
20. J. F. Eggleston, M. J. Galton and M. E. Jones, *Processes and Products of Science Teaching*, Schools Council Research Series (1976).
21. G. Monger, *Nuffield O Level Biology Continuation Report: Report for the need for revision of the Nuffield O level biology materials*, mimeographed (1971).
22. Nuffield Foundation, *Synopsis of the Biology Course, op. cit.*
23. *Ibid.*
24. J. F. Kerr, *The Problem of Curriculum Reform* (1967), also reprinted in J. F. Kerr (ed.), *Changing the Curriculum* (1968).
25. Nuffield Foundation, *Synopsis of the Biology Course, op. cit.*

26. Monger, *op. cit.*
27. T. Becher and S. Maclure, *The Politics of Curriculum Change* (1978).
28. P. H. Hirst, *Knowledge and the Curriculum* (1974).
29. Kerr (ed), *Changing the Curriculum, op. cit.*
30. *Ibid.*
31. Schools Council, 'Schools Council 18th Research Programme Studies based on the N and F proposals', in *Report of the Science Syllabus Steering Group to the Joint Examinations Sub-committee of the Schools Council*, mimeographed (1977).
32. Association for Science Education. *Alternatives for Science Education, A Consultative Document* (1979).
33. Kerr, *Curriculum Reform, op. cit.*
34. P. H. Hirst, 'The contribution of philosophy to the study of the curriculum', in Kerr (ed), *Changing the Curriculum, op. cit.*
35. D. Barnes, *Communication to Curriculum* (1976).
36. J. Britton, *Language and Learning* (1970).
37. N. Martin *et al.*, *Writing and Learning across the Curriculum* (1976).
38. M. Shayer, 'Conceptual demands in the Nuffield O level physics course', in *School Science Review*, LIV (1972), 26–34.
39. C. R. Sutton, *Teacher Education Project*. Trials material available from School of Education, 21 University Road, Leicester; Becher and Maclure, *op. cit.*
40. Kelly, *op. cit.*
41. *Schools Council Integrated Science Project* (1973).
42. A. Bullock, 'Science – a tarnished image?', in *School Science Review*, LVII, 201 (June 1976), 621.
43. P. J. Kelly, *Science, Life and Education*, inaugural lecture, University of London, mimeographed (1977).
44. *Ibid.*
45. Monger, *op. cit.*
46. Association for Science Education, *op. cit.*
47. Becher and Maclure, *op. cit.*

4 Curriculum evaluation and the traditional paradigm

MAURICE GALTON

In recent years probably more has been written about the subject of curriculum evaluation than all other aspects of curriculum theory combined. As the number of curriculum development projects have declined so more of the literature has been concerned with the theory rather than the practice of the evaluator's art. There are now many more people writing about how to evaluate than actually evaluating.

The trouble, of course, is that telling people 'how to evaluate' is addictive. Just like drug taking one easily gets 'hooked' on it without realizing that there is a problem. And just as a drug taker's ramblings become even more fanciful as the chemicals are absorbed into brain cells, so too do the outpourings of the evaluator sometimes become less coherent as the addiction takes hold. Thus the conventional curriculum process model, a diagram of a tetrahedron with 'objectives', 'content', 'learning experiences' and 'evaluation' at the corners, becomes a 'three dimensional representation in tri-polar space'. An arrangement of data in rows and columns is described as a 'two-way functional matrix'. And so it goes on. There are 'objectives', 'intended learning outcomes', 'intents', each new definition having just enough in common with previous ones to confuse the reader and confirm cynics in their opinion that one should never worry about missing out on the latest evaluation theory because like the trains, there will be another along after a short interval.

At first sight therefore, the author of the following passage appears to be a suitable case for treatment since judged on its initial impact the symptoms would indicate a high level of evaluation addiction. The writer, Professor Wiley,[1] begins,

> In order to help conceptualise the evaluation process it is useful to distinguish certain elements by labelling them with special terms. To these elements I have given the names: standards, objects, vehicles, and instruments . . .
>
> The main problem of evaluation, then, is to establish the effects of the *objects* on the *vehicles* by means of the *instruments*. The other element of the process is to compare these effects with the *standards*.

A first reaction, particularly among teachers, might be to dismiss such writing as indicative of the jargon which litters the field of curriculum evaluation. A second response might be to look for defects in one's own thought processes in case one had missed the point of an argument more subtle than at first realized. The professor, after all, enjoys an international reputation. Standards might be something more than just an alternative term to describe what some three years earlier Scriven called 'goals of evaluation' where the curriculum developer seeks to 'justify the weights given to objectives used to guide the development of the new curriculum material'.[2] Vehicles turn out to be another name for the pupils and the instruments are the data-collecting procedures. For some, a further source of possible confusion lies in the use of the word 'object' to describe the curriculum content when the word 'objective' is commonly used to describe behavioural outcomes. It would appear that Professor Wiley has gone out of his way to make life as difficult as possible for the reader.

It is not until the subsequent discussion at the end of the paper that the writer's intentions become more readily apparent. It seems that Professor Wiley has entered on what at first sight appears to be a somewhat abortive exercise in semantics with a particular purpose in mind. When asked about the need for these new definitions he argues that the old ones are inappropriate when making judgments about new curricula because evaluation

> is a substantive area fundamentally distinct from experimental psychology and the objects of interest are objects in the sense I've used . . . The main thrust and focus of the research in this area is not concerned with the same kind of phenomenon that experimental psychology is. Consequently we have to have different names.[3]

The detailed argument thus runs as follows. Evaluation studies have largely failed because instead of developing analytical methods specially for the purpose, evaluators have tried to apply techniques borrowed from the main stream of experimental psychology. Thus, for example, while the basic unit of study in experimental psychology is the individual, in evaluation we are concerned with groups rather than individual differences, which points to the use of class means as the unit of measurement. Professor Wiley instances the case of using item sampling, in which test items are randomly distributed in each class and the mean item score for each group of pupils is made the basis of the analysis. Besides being more efficient the method is also novel in that, since chance dictates which pupil takes which item, each mean will consist of a different sample of pupils' scores which are then generalizable to the class population. What is not clear, however, in his argument, is the reasoning behind the claim that in order to make such advances we need first to invent new terms and symbols. What appears to have happened among some curriculum evaluators is a loss of nerve at the repeated failure of past studies. There are those such as Schutz[4] who simply wish to write off completely previous work on evaluation based on what he calls the methods of 'psychologist-agronomist-biologist' which he brands as 'sick science'. In its place Schutz advocates the leap forward in search of new paradigms which will enable researchers to look at the whole evaluation problem in a new light. While Professor Wiley appears unwilling to abandon traditional analytical techniques entirely, he is clearly strongly attracted to the view that no progress will be made until there is radical rethinking about the nature of the models used to describe evaluation processes. These new definitions are intended to help create a climate in which this reorientation can be carried out.

In this country the main attack on more traditional types of evaluation has come from Parlett and Hamilton.[5] Their paper has become an essential element in the manifesto of the 'new wave' of curriculum theorists so that no book setting out alternative approaches to evaluation is complete without reprinting a modified version of the original text.[6]

Although Parlett and Hamilton integrate their various criticisms of traditional evaluation into one general argument, it is perhaps easier to discuss their objections if they are examined in two parts. The first type of objection concerns the use of *before* and *after* research designs, classed as 'true' experiments by Campbell and Stanley.[7] These, Parlett and Hamilton claim, are artificial, unethical, and unduly expensive. They are also, of course, very rare in educational research and Parlett and Hamilton are therefore forced to cite, as their two examples to criticize, a Swedish mathematics study[8] and the comparison of the Initial Teaching Alphabet with traditional orthography.[9] Experimental research is where the researcher arranges for a variation in, for example, a teaching method and then attempts to assess its effects. In practice most evaluation data is collected through descriptive survey evidence where the variation in methods, the use of different curricular materials, and their effects are observed within the classroom as they happen without any attempt to alter the situation by arranging who gets each set of materials, as in an experiment. In descriptive surveys relationships between different variables can be demonstrated by the use of correlational techniques, but unlike experimental research surveys cannot explain which of the variables affects the other. Attempts to set up any large-scale experimental study are often doomed to failure from the beginning, precisely because teachers easily perceive the problems and dangers described by Parlett and Hamilton, particularly the constraints on their teaching, and will thus have none of it. Most experimental studies are therefore small-scale ones, as for example, those designed to evaluate the success of discovery learning approaches.[10] It is for these reasons that Rosenshine and Furst[11] advocate the use of a research methodology which they term the 'correlational-experimental loop' where large-scale 'naturalistic' survey studies are followed by small-scale experimental ones, designed to demonstrate the causal links between specific variables, which the survey data, because of high correlations, suggests are important in the teaching-learning process.

Indeed what Parlett and Hamilton describe as the artificiality and weakness of experimental research has been frequently discussed by psychologists under the twin headings of *internal* and *external* validity. A wide range of problems and difficulties are listed for example by Barber.[12] His conclusion is not to abandon such experiments but to design them with greater care. It is also precisely because experimental studies may be atypical of classroom conditions that Rosenshine argues that they should be used in conjunction with naturalistic ones.

In the specific area of curriculum evaluation similar kinds of arguments have been rehearsed in the 'great debate' between Cronbach[13] and Scriven[14] which has become something of a historical classic. Put simply, Cronbach's argument is for more studies of the naturalistic survey type where questions about which variable causes which effect are regarded as relatively unimportant. Cronbach sees the research and development programme for bringing about curriculum change as similar in principle to that used to build and market a new make of car. If the manufacturer is interested in meeting the demand for a five-seater family vehicle with plenty of space for luggage and the dog, then he will build a model to these specifications. When it comes to buying the new car, the purchaser with a wife and three children will be uninterested in making comparisons with the performance of a two-seater sports model designed for a single man with his beautiful companion. In the same way comparisons between the old and new curriculum are equally irrelevant, according to Cronbach, because they have been developed with different needs in mind. The important question to be answered is whether the new curriculum meets the specifications around which it was designed.

Scriven, however, would argue that comparative studies were still important, particularly in the case where two alternative makes of car with similar specifications are available. He suggests, perhaps rather fancifully, that if an alternative curriculum is not available it should be rapidly designed by graduate students in order to provide a 'placebo' for a comparative study. He argues that it would be wrong to abandon all comparative evaluations because in the past so many have failed to demonstrate important differences. The fact that there may be no difference between two different treatments, in this case two curriculum packages, is not necessarily unimportant since if pupils following different curriculum courses obtain similar examination results, other factors such as their relative enjoyment, the cost and time of mounting each course would then become even more decisive elements in any final decision about which package to adopt.

Scriven clearly recognizes the need for descriptive information at the development stage as well as comparative studies. He and those who advocate experimental comparative evaluation designs would claim that the question of *what* and *how much* pupils learn as a result of receiving a course of instruction must continue to be one of the important elements in any enquiry about the effectiveness of different curricular packages. Some of this evidence will be gathered through surveys during the *formative* stage when the curriculum package is being developed, so that it can be fed back to those responsible for developing the curriculum units. But at some point *summative* judgments are required in which some of the important effects, isolated from the earlier descriptive survey studies, are subjected to testing under experimental conditions which attempts to discover their possible causes.

Such studies, for all the reasons given by Parlett and Hamilton, are never likely to be other than small-scale ones and as Rosenshine and Furst suggest they should be designed to test the results of larger-scale survey research which in the case of a curriculum development would be carried out at the formative stage. To cite the case of the Science 5–13 evaluation[15] as pointing to the failure of traditional experimental designs is somewhat unfair.[16] These researchers started their study at the opposite end of the 'correlational-experimental loop' and attempted a comparative evaluation before having first obtained a wide enough data base through descriptive studies at the formative stage. When the findings were presented they were thus unable to interpret their conclusions to the developers within a general context.

Thus Parlett and Hamilton's criticisms are not new ones and have long been recognized by those who advocate the use of experimental designs within educational research. Insofar as experimental research can be used in evaluation it has a limited application, as reflected by the absence of such designs in a summary of the different approaches employed by most of the recent British evaluation studies.[17] Parlett and Hamilton's critique of experimental research is an eloquent one and, since it is couched in layman's language, it may be seen as helpful in clarifying the issues for those with a limited understanding of psychometric techniques. In that, by overstating the case, it appears to suggest that experimental studies are an alternative rather than a complementary technique within an overall evaluation strategy, it goes further than most advocates of psychometric methods and, in this respect, is therefore misleading.

Turning to the second part of the case against traditional forms of evaluation, the other type of objection is closely integrated within these criticisms of experimental design research. Parlett and Hamilton argue that in such designs the effectiveness of the curriculum package is generally assessed by 'objective' rather than 'subjective' or 'impressionistic' information. The juxtaposition of two very different types of criticism encourages the reader to fall into the trap of reasoning that since experimental evaluations often seek to quantify information, aimed at making them 'objective', and since experimental evaluations have been shown to be artificial, it therefore follows that the quantifying information is also likely to be artificial, leading to superficial treatment of the more salient features of the innovation under investigation. But, as we have seen, experimental studies are often artificial not because they use 'objective' measures, but because they tend to be atypical of normal classroom conditions.

Parlett and Hamilton argue that in place of these so-called objective measures, such as tests and questionnaires, the main data gathering technique for what they call 'illuminative evaluation' should consist of impressionistic, 'subjective' accounts of the introduction of the new curriculum package into the classroom. Hamilton,[18] in a later paper, expands on these points in arguing for the use of these impressionistic classroom accounts in place of interaction analysis, the alternative observation strategy for collecting information about the classroom *process*.

The inclusion of process data in evaluation studies has been generally recognized as an important but neglected feature of the methodology.[19] During the 1960s writers on evaluation tended to view the classroom as a 'black box' in which the new curriculum package was fed in at one end to emerge at the other, relatively unscathed by its treatment at the hands of the teacher and the pupils. A number of studies have shown, however, that both teachers and pupils react to the new materials in a variety of different ways.[20] Indeed, in the case of the Nuffield Science schemes, teachers were particularly encouraged to modify and adapt the materials to their own requirements. This interaction between the teacher and the pupils and the curriculum materials should be a factor in determining the effectiveness of the package, particularly in respect of *products*, the attainment and attitudes of the pupils. What therefore is required is a 'glass box' model of evaluation where such interactions are observed as part of the study. Where this has been done, then there is evidence that failure to establish significant differences is less likely.[21] It would seem then, that the worst fears of these gloomy illuminators do not always materialize.

Two types of observation techniques can be used to monitor the use of the curriculum package within the classroom. Systematic observation or interaction analysis,[22] as it is sometimes called, requires an observer to code behaviour at regular intervals according to a series of pre-specified categories. Participant observation is based on an observer's impressionistic account of classroom events. It is claimed that a participant observer, because he carries no preconceived set of ideas about what should or should not be recorded, is best able to describe just what it feels like to be part of the process under study. In systematic observation the coder is expected to be like a 'fly on the wall' and remain relatively uninvolved in the events taking place. A participant observer, however, aims to take an active part in the proceedings so that, in the case of a classroom, for example, it should be possible to describe what it would be like to be taught by the particular teacher, or what it would be like to teach particular pupils. Parlett and Hamilton favour the participant approach. According to them the illuminative evaluator is 'cautious in the deployment of (systematic) techniques. In that they record only surface behaviour they do not facilitate the uncovering of underlying, more meaningful features.'[23]

In his more wide-ranging criticisms of systematic observation Hamilton repeats this charge. Clearly such writers must have some prior knowledge about what these meaningful features of classrooms are to make so bold an assertion. As McIntyre[24] points out, if those who seek to quantify their observations also shared in this secret knowledge then there would be little need to justify the use of specific categories. McIntyre argues that while it is true that systematic observation must result in less than a full description of classroom activity this is the case 'whoever the observer and however he observes'. The issue therefore is not 'whether information is neglected but rather how it is determined what information will be neglected'. In systematic observation the categories are defined in such a way to ensure that any two observers will agree when coding a particular classroom event. This at least makes it possible for others to appreciate the consequences of the decision to collect only certain kinds of information. It is in this sense that they are said to be 'objective'. Because the participant observer makes his selection of events while present in the classroom such decisions are not accessible to the outsider so that no such objective appraisal can be made.

Hamilton also complains that observational research, like traditional evaluation, is over-concerned with quantification and with seeking statistical generalizations. While again, as McIntyre points out, participant observers also seem very prone to make quantitative statements, the basis of which are often far from clear, it can be argued that this very property of systematic observation, with its precise generalizations following on from careful statistical analysis, is its very strength, making it so appropriate for use in evaluation studies.

Once a 'glass box' approach to evaluation is adopted it becomes essential to discuss the use of the curriculum package within the context of specific hypotheses about the effect of certain teaching behaviours on pupils' classroom learning. While the 'new wave' of curriculum theorists have performed a useful service in pointing out that there are other participants who are concerned in the process of curriculum renewal beside developers, teachers and pupils, it nevertheless ought to remain true that a major concern for any evaluation should be the operation of the package within the classroom in accordance with the original intentions of its makers. Thus the Nuffield Science scheme sought to foster an 'enquiry' approach both in the way teachers taught and in the manner pupils learned. This in turn suggests that a high proportion of interactions between teachers and pupils should consist of statements and questions requiring the *interpretation* of observed data, the *design* of experimental procedures and the formulation of hypotheses rather than with the transmission of factual information.

The incidence of such distinct categories of behaviour can be carefully monitored using systematic observation instruments such as STOS, the Science Teaching Observation Schedule.[25] Analysis of STOS data suggests that less than a quarter of science teachers adopted even the semblance of an enquiry approach. Much of the emphasis in teaching was still largely on teacher-directed rather that pupil-initiated activity concerned mainly with factual presentation rather than problem-solving or hypothesis-testing. Had such information been in the hands of the curriculum developers before they embarked on constructing the new package, it would have been of immeasurable value and could possibly have led to their rethinking the whole approach.

In spite of the small number of teachers who used a pupil-centred enquiry approach subsequent analysis suggested that in biology, and to a lesser extent physics, the use of such teaching tactics enabled pupils to outperform those taught didactically on tests designed to measure higher order cognitive skills such as problem-solving and data manipulation.[26] The STOS study was able to show that over 40 per cent of possible differences in attainment and attitude were linked directly with teaching style. Higher percentages might have been obtained if the attainment tests had discriminated among the less able pupils. Nevertheless this is a better success rate than normally achieved in comparative evaluations using a black box model. It suggests that, if traditional designs are modified to take account of the effects of teacher-pupil interaction, they can provide valuable information for curriculum developers. Thus, in retrospect, Professor Wiley has perhaps been too pessimistic in his decision to abandon evaluation techniques developed from the main stream of psychology. What is at issue here is not the ultimate goal of creating a practical theory of teaching and learning within which context new curriculum packages can be evaluated, but the methods to be used to make this revolutionary advance.

The notion of the 'two faces of science' should not lead us into the error of thinking that the creative researcher hacking away at the frontiers of knowledge is a different kind of animal from those filling in contours and boundaries on the map behind, the latter tending to build upon and improve existing practices. Pure science has two important things to tell us in the matter of revolutionary discovery. First, that rival theories if developed by the yard-stick of scientific objectivity are often merged into a more comprehensive framework at a later date when many of the earlier arguments are shown up as irrelevant. The debate between the corpuscular and wave theories of light provides an apt illustration of this point and nearer home the sterility of much of the debate between the 'gestalt' and 'behaviourist' schools of psychology offers a warning of danger in advancing to positions on the basis of the 'inspired guesses' without an adequate earlier framework based upon the analysis of objective data.

In the same way much of the confrontation between the 'new wave' and the traditional evaluators and more particularly between participant and systematic observers can also now be seen as unproductive. Stufflebeam's 'decision-making model',[27] Stake's attempt at 'responsive evaluation'[28] and nearer home McDonald's 'holistic approach'[29] all have important things to teach traditional evaluators in the matter of formative evaluation techniques which are responsive to the needs of different clienteles. At the same time many of the studies, particularly those using participant observation, as McIntyre in another context also observes, fail to move from a position of generating interesting hypotheses to a point where these can be verified by the use of more systematic research procedures.

More important perhaps, the second lesson to be learned from pure science is that the basis of much scientific progress has been through technological advance which has provided new types of data-gathering instrument. When such advances are made it has often been because the greater precision afforded by these new techniques has allowed old data to be reworked as a result of making observations of finer detail. The progression from Galileo's telescope to the latest radio instruments illustrates the point well in astronomy. Examination of any scientific journal over the last 50 years will testify to the influence of improved data-gathering instruments on the progress of research. In chemistry, for example, the same systems have continued to be studied by a variety of techniques from the early mass spectrograph to the latest electron spin resonance machine, each in turn giving a more detailed picture of the underlying chemical structure by uncovering the more complex mechanisms of each reaction.

It is therefore incumbent on us to think very seriously before seeking to abandon existing research models. Before doing so we should be clear in our own minds that failure is due to the weakness of the model rather than the imperfection of the measuring device, that possible modifications to the model are likely to prove equally abortive and that the data-gathering instruments already available have been developed to their utmost capacity. In the case of those arguing so strongly for a new revolutionary approach to curriculum evaluation and the complete abandonment of the existing traditional paradigm, there is little evidence to show that all these things have yet been done. For Professor Wiley to argue for the use of the class as the sole sampling unit in curriculum evaluation puts on him an obligation to specify the kind of information we should need to collect about the transactions taking place within the classroom and to suggest in what ways this would differ from the data now collected. He would also need to go further and suggest the appropriate data-gathering instruments which will be required to obtain reliable information of the kind he has in mind. It is only through doing this that we can perhaps begin to overcome some of the inherent weaknesses within existing traditional evaluation designs.

Already one important modification has been the collection of process as well as product data in more recent evaluation studies. One factor in this advance has been the development of a wide range of different systematic observation systems designed to mirror the intentions of the curriculum developer. This has allowed us to add to our knowledge in a very precise way regarding the use of the curriculum package within different classrooms where differing teaching strategies are used. In early studies researchers made use of systems such as Flander's FIAC[30] which reflected a stage of development in evaluation corresponding to Galileo's telescope in astronomy. Critics such as Hamilton tend to write off the whole of interaction analysis as if this were still the case. Yet a recent anthology of British classroom observation instruments shows that there are 41 different schedules, of which only three bear the slightest resemblance to Flanders' original instrument.[31] Indeed it is the wide variety of these systems which make it possible to monitor behaviour even in the most informally organized classroom, which is a striking feature of British classroom research.

Where further urgent advance is now required is in the matter of the product measures used in comparative type evaluations. Evaluators working outside the traditional framework tend to ignore this aspect of curriculum altogether. But as we move into the 1980s it is difficult to see how, with the setting up of the Assessment of Performance Unit following the demands for greater accountability, this position can continue to be tenable.[32] It is also generally acknowledged that the early evaluations, by using norm-referenced tests created a situation where the initial attainment of the pupils was certain to account for a greater proportion of the post-test variation than would the use of different curriculum packages.[33] The suggestion that criterion-referenced items are more appropriate, while generally accepted, has not been matched by efficient technological development to enable appropriate tests to be constructed. As with evaluation more people write about the need for criterion-referenced measurement than actually concern themselves with producing valid and reliable items.[34]

However, the needs of the A.P.U. and the development of item-banking techniques[35] has at least brought the discussion down to practical matters and although there is considerable argument about the validity of the newer assessment techniques, many of the issues are clear cut and open to empirical testing.[36] There is every likelihood that this will be done within the next few years, and the range of assessment techniques then available to the evaluator will be far more precise and relevant to the aims of each particular curriculum. Both systematic observation and item-banking offer evaluators, for the first time, data-gathering techniques which can provide objective, reliable and valid information about teachers and pupils in the context of using new curricular material. At the moment there is still considerable scope for refinement in these data-gathering instruments with consequent improvement in their precision which should make possible even more effective evaluations at both formative and summative stages. It is to be hoped that those evaluators who are at present so sceptical of any further advance within the traditional framework of the behavioural sciences will begin to recognize the power of some of these new techniques and incorporate them within their own evaluation paradigms.

1. D. E. Wiley, 'The design and analysis of evaluation studies', in M. C. Wittrock and D. E. Wiley (eds), *The Evaluation of Instruction: Issues and problems* (New York, 1970), 261–2.
2. M. Scriven, 'The methodology of evaluation', in *A.E.R.A. Monograph No. 1* (1967), 39–84.
3. Wiley, *op. cit.*, 278.
4. R. E. Schutz, 'Methodological issues in curriculum research', in *Review of Educational Research*, XXXIX (1969), 359–66.
5. M. Parlett and D. Hamilton, 'Evaluation as illumination: a new approach to the study of innovatory programs', in *Occasional Paper*, 9 (1972).
6. M. Parlett and D. Hamilton, 'Evaluation as illumination: a new approach to the study of innovatory programs', in D. Tawney (ed.), *Curriculum Evaluation Today: Trends and implications*, Schools Council Research Series (1976), M. Parlett and D. Hamilton, 'Evaluation as illumination: a new approach to the study of innovatory programs', in D. Hamilton *et al.* (eds), *Beyond the Numbers Game* (1977).

7. D. T. Campbell and J. C. Stanley, 'Experimental and quasi-experimental designs for research on teaching', in N. L. Gage (ed.), *Handbook of Research on Teaching* (1963).
8. I. Larsson, *Individualised Mathematics Teaching* (Stockholm, 1973).
9. J. A. Downing (ed.), *The i.t.a. Symposium*, N.F.E.R. (1967).
10. W. S. Anthony, 'Learning rules by discovery', in *Journal of Educational Psychology*, LXIV (1973), 325–8.
11. B. Rosenshine and N. Furst, 'The use of direct observation to study teaching', in R. M. W. Travers (ed.), *Second Handbook of Research on Teaching* (1973).
12. T. X. Barber, 'Pitfalls in research: nine investigator and experimenter effects', in Travers, *op. cit.*
13. L. J. Cronbach, 'Course improvement through evaluation', in *Teachers College Record*, LXIV (1963), 672–83.
14. Scriven, *op. cit.*
15. W. Harlen, *Science 5–13: A formative evaluation*, Schools Council Research Series (1975).
16. L. Stenhouse, *An Introduction to Curriculum Research and Development* (1975), 105.
17. M. Eraut, 'Some recent evaluation studies of curriculum projects – a review', in Tawney, *op. cit.*
18. D. Hamilton and S. Delamont, 'Classroom research: a cautionary tale', in *Research in Education*, XI (1974), 1–5.
19. R. E. Stake, 'Towards a technology for the evaluation of educational programs', in *A.E.R.A. Monograph No. 1* (1967), 1–12; J. F. Eggleston and M. J. Galton, 'Interaction analysis and evaluation', in *Paedagogica Europaea*, VIII (1973), 122–31.
20. J. J. Gallagher, 'Teacher variation in concept presentation on BSCS Curriculum Program', *B.S.C.S. Newsletter*, XXX (1967).
21. M. J. Galton and J. F. Eggleston, 'Some characteristics of effective science teaching', *European Journal of Science Education*, I (1978), 75–85; R. P. Tisher, 'The nature of verbal discourse in classrooms', in W. J. Campbell (ed.), *Scholars in Context: The effects of environment on learning* (Sydney, 1970).
22. M. J. Galton, 'Interaction analysis', in R. McAleese and D. Unwin (eds), *Encyclopaedia of Educational Media Communications and Technology* (1978), 418–40.
23. Parlett and Hamilton, *Occasional Paper, op. cit.*, 20.
24. D. McIntyre and G. MacLeod, 'The characteristics and uses of systematic classroom observation', in R. McAleese and D. Hamilton (eds), *Understanding Classroom Life*, N.F.E.R. (1978).
25. J. F. Eggleston, M. J. Galton and M. E. Jones, *A Science Teaching Observation Schedule*, Schools Council Research Series (1975).

26. J. F. Eggleston, M. J. Galton and M. E. Jones, *Processes and Products of Science Teaching*, Schools Council Research Series (1976).

27. D. L. Stufflebeam, 'Evaluation as enlightenment for decision-making', in W. H. Beatty (ed.), *Improving Educational Assessment and an Inventory of Affective Behaviour*, National Education Association (Washington, D.C., 1969).

28. R. E. Stake, 'The countenance of educational evaluation', in *Teachers College Record*, LXVIII (1967), 523–40.

29. B. McDonald, 'The evaluation of the Humanities Curriculum Project: a holistic approach', in *Theory into Practice*, X (1971), 163–7.

30. N. A. Flanders, 'Teacher influence on pupil attitudes and achievement', in *Cooperative Research Programme Project*, CCCLXXXXVII (Minneapolis, 1960).

31. M. J. Galton, *British Mirrors: A collection of classroom observation systems* (1978).

32. M. J. Galton, 'Accountability and the teacher: some moves and countermoves', in C. Richards (ed.), *Power and the Curriculum* (1978).

33. J. F. Eggleston, 'Measuring attainment for curriculum evaluation', in H. E. MacIntosh (ed.), *Techniques and Problems of Assessment* (1974).

34. R. Sumner and T. S. Robertson, *Criterion-Referenced Measurement and Criterion-Referenced Tests*, N.F.E.R. (1977).

35. B. Choppin, *Item Banking and the Monitoring of Achievement*, N.F.E.R. (1978).

36. H. Goldstein and S. Blinkhorn, 'Monitoring educational standards – an inappropriate model', in *Bulletin of the British Psychological Society*, XXX (1977).

5 From innovation to adaptability: the changing perspective of curriculum development

PETER KELLY

The word *nous* has a particular fascination. It is derived from Ancient Greek and was used by Plato in reference to the intellect and a mode of thought which today we would label as scientific or rational. On the other hand *nous* has a colloquial meaning which was drawn to my attention some years back by Jack Kerr. In northern England the words stands for common sense and gumption: a blend of practical and moral purpose with a high load of intuition and motivation.

The word fascinates me because its two meanings are so often seen as opposites as when intellectual theories are scorned by practitioners and, in reverse, when the irrationalities of our social behaviour prompt us to call for more systematic, scientific planning. Yet, although we might polarize in debate between rationality and common sense, the real world of social action has an essentially holistic character to which, to my mind, the word *nous* can reasonably be applied. Surely effective social action is derived from an approach which combines the steadiness of intellectual rationality with the flair of intuition and the impetus of motivation.

In this essay I am concerned with curriculum development, a form of social action; and it seems to me appropriate that I should examine it with a *nous* perspective, attempting to be rational without straining the bounds of common sense. In so doing I suspect I will be reflecting an attitude which Jack Kerr would wish to bear on the subject.

A TIME FOR INNOVATION

They were *nous*-like decisions which, in the 1960s, established the early national curriculum development projects in Britain. There was a widespread view that courses and teaching methods were out-of-date. There were strong supporting pressures from society for reform, and demands for something significant to happen. It was a time for innovation.

The word innovation, as it was applied to the curricula of our schools, had a special meaning in those days. Primarily it was about reform: changing things for the better. There was a surprising consensus on what was needed and, even when there were differing opinions about what was better, there was little doubt that, whatever it was, it ought to be achieved.

The curriculum development projects were seen as innovative also in the sense that they had something new to offer in terms of curriculum content, teaching and learning methods and curriculum materials. Occasionally genuine original ideas were introduced, but mainly the products of the projects were new in being different associations of old ideas or new to the time and circumstances in which the projects existed.

Above all the innovations were identifiable. Some were, in effect, packages of books, visual aids, equipment and instructions for teachers and pupils. At the other extreme, some were purely a set of ideas aimed at stimulating teachers to introduce their own innovations. There was a great variety but in each case it was possible to identify the particular innovation developed by a project. Certainly it was invariably the intention of the members of a project, and those that sponsored it, that their innovation be clearly visible.

There was, then, little that was subtle about curriculum development in the 1960s. It was a large-scale, publicly declared attempt to solve what were seen as large-scale and pressing national educational problems. It was the view that the reforms needed to be initiated outside the schools and passed on to them. The traditional respect for the autonomy of schools in curriculum matters was observed, and there was no talk of obligations; but it was not accepted that schools would reform themselves.

The model of curriculum development employed was of the centre-to-periphery type. Courses were developed by relatively small, selected groups of 'experts'* and made available to the schools where they were expected to be implemented. It was assumed that provided the products of the projects had sufficient virtue and appeal then their adoption would be automatic.

The projects were carefully planned and usually involved pilot studies, field testing and evaluation. Rarely, however, were the problems of disseminating ideas and materials to schools, and of implementing them within schools which had not taken part in trials, fully considered. It

---

*These were not experts in curriculum development because there had been little experience of it previously. Members of the groups were 'expert' in being outstanding teachers, text book writers, examiners or having some other associated expertise.

was, for example, not until 1972 that the Schools Council (some eight years after its foundation) established a Working Party on Dissemination.

THE IMPACT OF INNOVATION

In the mid-1970s Jan Harding, Robert Nicodemus and myself undertook a study of the extent to which innovations in science education produced by various Nuffield and Schools Council Projects had been used by schools.[1] We found that, typically, most of the schools taking up a project's products did so within five years of them becoming commercially available.* Following this initial burst, the curve of uptake tended to flatten out. After 10 years or so, whilst some schools still take up the innovations, newcomers are few in number.

After an innovation had been on the market for about five years, a majority (possibly up to 80 per cent) of teachers eligible to use it knew about the innovation and considered that their work had been influenced to some extent by it, utilizing at least some of the ideas and materials involved. However, only a minority (possibly 10–20 per cent) were committed sufficiently to consider themselves as fully adopting the innovation and not all of these implemented it faithfully. Most of these teachers introduced new subject matter and used new procedures but rarely did they change their teaching style. The degree of change tended to be an extension of previous practice rather than to differ from it or to be a reorientation of it.

CURRICULUM DIFFUSION

Clearly then, there was a disparity between the expectations of the curriculum development projects and the depth of their influence on the curriculum of schools and the practice of teachers. This is now widely recognized and, of course, it is important that we know something about how this disparity arose. This leads us to consider what may be called curriculum diffusion. The term, in a general sense, refers to the spread of materials, ideas, values, attitudes and behaviour related to the school curriculum from one location to another. Here, more specifically, we can use it to refer to the spread of innovations from a curriculum development project.

Curriculum diffusion, I suggest, is not the same as curriculum dissemination. This is the term I would apply to the strategies and activities by which it is *intended* that an innovation be passed on. The term

---

*The generalized statements here are derived from data collected by the Curriculum Diffusion Research Project. It should be pointed out that there is variation hidden by the statements. Data from a wider range of projects are given in the Schools Council Impact and Take-up Project Report.[2]

diffusion refers to what actually happens; to the interaction between dissemination and the complex of influences in the social context in which it occurs. At the same time it is a continuing process and, for example, can relate as much to the movement of ideas in the development phase of a project as it does to the effects of the dissemination initiated after development.

A portrayal of dissemination depicts systematic administration, meetings, plans drawn up on paper, timetables, the distribution of newsletters, organized in-service courses, and even a computer or two. Invariably it will have four inter-related aspects. The movement of people and materials to implement an innovation (translocation); the passage of information about an innovation through printed or oral media and personal contact (communication); the provision of stimuli for change, either externally induced or self-generated (motivation); and the development of the considerable understanding and commitment required for the effective implementation of an innovation (re-education).

Diffusion includes such things, but also aspects such as the burden of ever-filling in-trays; our varied perceptions of what we know, of what we think we know, and of our ignorances; the ponderous and ephemeral decision-making which occurs in committees, in staff-rooms and in classrooms; and the interplay of our domestic and professional lives. Diffusion, then, involves a mix of both ordered and disordered personal and social activity.

Let me hasten to add that curriculum diffusion is not an analogue of chemical diffusion. There is rather more to it than that. If anything the Oxford Dictionary gets very close to the sense of the term: diffuse (vt) diffusion (n): send forth, shed abroad (light, particles, heat, geniality, knowledge, rumour). One certainly is concerned with particles (ideas or materials) and, hopefully, knowledge. Most times there is geniality but it does get heated, and rumour is ever present!

AMBIVALENCE IN DISSEMINATION

Parallel to the studies of the uptake of innovations from projects in science education referred to earlier, we also looked at some of the diffusion processes which affected this uptake. The backcloth to these studies of diffusion was an examination of dissemination. The projects had two main targets for their dissemination strategies, teachers in schools and supporting agencies such as L.E.A.s, examination boards, equipment manufacturers and head teachers. However, their aims for dissemination were rarely spelt out and there was uncertainty about what they should be, and considerable uncertainty about what they should be seen to be. We categorized them as follows:

Adoptive aims: which intend that teachers will adopt an innovation and implement it faithfully.

Adaptive aims: which intend that teachers will adapt some aspects of an innovation to their current practice. This is often expressed as a compromise between the 'ideals' of the innovation and the 'realities' which a teacher has to contend with.

Innovative aims: which intend that the dissemination of an innovation will act as a stimulus for further innovation and, in this sense, foster the professional development of a teacher.

Instrumental aims: which encourage the achievement of adoptive, adaptive or innovative aims by indirect means; for example, changing examinations and tests in order to encourage changes in courses.

The greatest uncertainty was with the first category for there was considerable reluctance to be seen to be imposing on, or dictating to, teachers. It was not because people in the projects would have been disturbed if all teachers had taken up their innovations fully, particularly as the views of teachers were frequently taken into account and the projects' team members were invariably teachers on secondment. It was that the social norm of teacher autonomy in curriculum matters was so firmly entrenched in the educational mind. This was reflected also, for example, in the studied posture of neutrality towards the innovations adopted by bodies such as Her Majesty's Inspector (H.M.I.), the Association for Science Education (A.S.E.) and Examinations Boards. They were all co-operative but refrained from taking sides. Adaptive and innovative aims were much more acceptable.

Instrumental aims recognize the importance of a range of outside agencies, such as examination boards, which influence what is taught in schools. Now, if we compare instrumental aims, which were strongly accepted, with adoptive aims, which rarely were, we have a paradox. Whilst there was a reluctance by the project members to dictate to teachers directly it was considered less unreasonable to influence those agencies which strongly affected teachers and hence, in a sense, to dictate indirectly to teachers. It was an expression of the considerable ambivalence project teams and others had to dissemination.

L.E.A.s, examination boards, and others, such as colleges and universities, were among the intervening agencies between the development work of a project and its implementation. They were crucial agencies of dissemination, yet none were under the control of the projects and, in fact, the influence the projects could bring to bear on them was severely limited by their resources. Little funding was given to projects for dissemination because dissemination was seen as the particular responsibility of L.E.A.s. At the same time, the commitment of the L.E.A.s and other such dissemination agencies was often limited by their dilemma of not wanting to be seen to be supporting one innovation more than others or, on occasion, more than traditional practices.

There were also other dilemmas of a moral and logistic nature. Given a limited amount of money is it reasonable for a few schools to be given extra funds for implementing innovations whilst others, who would prefer merely to improve the quality of what they are already doing, get less? Should you anticipate teachers' possible interest in innovations and prepare extra budgeting for in-service courses, extra books and so on, or wait until they express interest? The former could waste money, the latter could result in low use of innovations.

Some L.E.A.s had well-organized dissemination strategies. Some did not and relied on *ad hoc* activities at the tactical level. Much depended on other people and other institutions.

Dissemination, of course, is a major input of the diffusion processes affecting the utilization of an innovation. The form it took in the diffusion of the innovations we considered clearly depended on the influence of prevailing educational philosophies and structures, and the balance of control and influence between the development projects and dissemination agents. A particular feature of this was the lowering of the commitment to change arising from unclear and ambivalent attitudes towards the practice of dissemination.

NEGATIVE REACTIONS

When the science development projects were first established in the early 1960s there were generally positive social attitudes towards them. Soon after their products were released and as further projects were initiated in the middle and late 1960s the social climate became less supportive. This was due, in part, to changes in public attitudes towards science. With the growth of environmental and other social concerns the status of science declined and environmental studies, humanities and other curriculum areas were accorded a greater balance of commitment and resources.

This process of depreciation as the social climate altered was mirrored in other changes. As more schools became aware of the innovations, discussion about constraints on implementation became more prevalent and the aims, content and activities of the innovations received less consideration. In a sense, also, the neutrality of various organizations towards the innovations, referred to earlier, aided depreciation. Their neutrality could be interpreted as lack of support and led to suspicions of implicit opposition. In fact this was recognized after a while and some of the bodies organized in-service courses and other activities concerned with the innovations although still retaining their neutral pose. The negative influences of these postures were not necessarily intended, nor were those of evaluation studies. However, the impetus of evaluation is frequently criticism, particularly when its purpose is to seek the improvement of the innovations. Furthermore as times changed, the frame of reference for judging the innovations changed and criticism became easier.

The new science curricula existed only for a period – say five or so years – in a conducive innovation climate. As time passed their diffusion became increasingly influenced by negative reactions.

DECISION-MAKING IN THE SCHOOLS

Within the schools decisions concerned with the use of the new curricula appeared to be essentially adventitious and circumstantial. Table 1 shows the relations between the intentions of a sample of teachers attending in-service courses for the Nuffield A-level Biological Science project and what they did one year later. In fact the relations are highly variable.

INTENTIONS

		To adopt early	To try out and then adopt	To try out	Considering trial	Total
	Adopted early	5	4	12	6	27
AFTER A YEAR	Adopted late	7	13	6	9	35
	Partial adoption	19	19	5	8	51
	Not adopted	11	2	7	9	29
	Totals	42	38	30	32	

Table 1. Intentions of 142 teachers towards adoption of the Nuffield A-level Biological Science project compared with what they had done one year later.[3]

My colleague Jan Harding looked at the process of decision making more closely through extensive interviews with teachers.[4] As a result we came to the view that the decision to adopt an innovation depended primarily on teachers being dissatisfied with their current situation. In addition there are matching processes by which teachers assess their perceptions of the needs of their pupils, their resources and organization, and their educational philosophy and teaching style with their perception of the comparable aspects of an innovation. This is depicted in

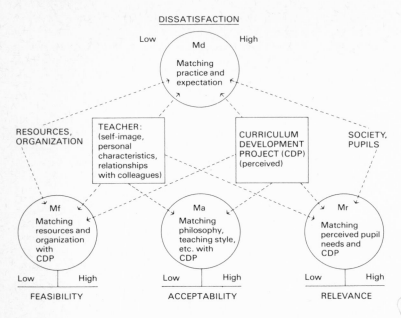

Figure 1. The processes of teacher decision-making in relation to curriculum innovations[5]

figure 1. Adoption is unlikely unless the innovation is assessed highly in each category.

These two slightly edited descriptions by Dr Harding of events in schools concerned with the Schools Council Integrated Science Project (SCISP) will illustrate how the matching processes operate.

In the first school, the head of science had heard about SCISP previously but it did not assume significance for him until the L.E.A. approached him offering financial support if the school took part in the dissemination phase of the project. Here was a two-fold pressure: the increased resources and the status and recognition of a trial school (he had experienced both in the Nuffield chemistry trials in a previous school). This disturbed his state of satisfaction (Md increased) and he and his colleagues went to considerable lengths to find out more about the project. They reported being favourably impressed by it (high Ma).

However, the situation in the science department was changing as the result of secondary reorganization. It had to accommodate extra pupils of lower, but unknown (to the school) ability in the year into which SCISP would have to be introduced. The project's materials were not developed for the whole ability range, and their interpretation of the social needs of the new pupils made the science staff reluctant to stream them on entry. The project thus had limited relevance (Mr), although it was feasible (Mf) to the extent that financial support was available and a member of staff was willing to organize the course. They were prepared to modify the materials but found that some of the later parts of the course were not then available (low Mf). So, in the event, the head of science, in consultation with his colleagues, decided 'to shelve' SCISP.

The head of science in the second school was dissatisfied with the way the energies of his department were fragmented over several unconnected courses and he was concerned by the lack of support offered to probationary teachers in these circumstances (high Md). The headmaster had recently cut the time available for science which created difficulties for courses in the separate sciences, i.e. biology, chemistry and physics (low Mf for current courses). SCISP required less time.

The head of science had visited trial schools and attended a three-day course to find out about SCISP. The social orientation of the project pleased him (Ma) and he saw it to be more relevant to the needs of his pupils (Mr). Financial support had been offered and time for departmental meetings included on the time-table (leading to high Mf for an integrated course). The local H.M.I. and Warden of the Curriculum Development Centre approved of SCISP (Md).

The high position on each matching dimension resulted in the decision to use SCISP.

These descriptions should not be taken as examples of large-scale patterns. In the schools it was the variety of the combinations of circumstances and the teachers' reaction to them which were most obvious. There was little evidence of broad, uni-directional patterns of influence. Mainly decisions emerged from unique circumstances and particular moments of time.

These descriptions of the ambivalence, changing circumstances and growing negativism which affected the diffusion of these curriculum innovations, together with an appreciation of the complexity of influences affecting decision-making in schools, whilst not giving the whole story, certainly explains to some extent how the gap between the intentions of developers and the reception of their work by schools arose. However, before we try to assess the implications of these findings let us look at the other side of the coin, at some of the unexpected positive outcomes of diffusion.

INCIDENTAL AND 'UNOFFICIAL' DIFFUSION

As we explored diffusion by case studies of local authorities and schools, and traced the channels of communication by which knowledge of curriculum innovation was passed on and through which activities concerned with the implementation of innovations were initiated, it became clear that much diffusion occurred incidentally and through 'unofficial' channels.

For example, in one area where there were trial schools of the Nuffield O-level biology project, it happened that some of the trial teachers were members of an examining group for the Certificate of Secondary Education (C.S.E.), an examination of lower standard than the General Certificate of Education (G.C.E.) for which the project was intended. However, the teachers were so convinced of the value of some of the innovations of the project and of their suitability for a wide range of pupils that they had them included in the syllabus for the C.S.E. examination before the development work of the project had been completed. It was a completely unforeseen and incidental outcome of the project's work.

In the L.E.A.s we studied it was not always the official L.E.A. adviser or channel of communication which was most influential. Temporary groups and 'unofficial' leadership played a significant part in the diffusion process. Active local groups of teachers sprang up led by enthusiastic individuals. Initiatives were taken by individual lecturers in colleges and universities; and local branches of scientific institutions and teachers' organizations, for example, also fostered activities. Indeed, in some areas L.E.A. advisers encouraged such 'unofficial' diffusion, seeing it as the most effective and economical dissemination strategy available to them.

ISSUES AND QUESTIONS

This experience of curriculum development and diffusion, covering some 15 years or so, begs many questions. It raises issues concerning the efficiency of the development and dissemination strategies employed and, indeed, of educational administration with respect to the curriculum. It highlights the problem of defining the role of teachers in curriculum development. It queries some of our cherished educational traditions with respect to the curriculum. From the many which could be asked I would like to concentrate on two questions.

Was the experience worth the time, effort and money spent on it?

What ideas for future curriculum development can be gleaned from this experience?

WAS IT WORTH IT?

An answer to this question will depend on the criterion you use for worth. If, for example, you disagree with the aims of projects clearly the answer is 'no'. However, certainly as far as the Nuffield science projects were concerned, there is evidence of considerable agreement with the aims, from Kerr's early study *Practical Work in School Science*[6] to studies and activities[7] when the projects were evolving. On the whole projects were pitched at the level of the ideals of most teachers. Yet, even accepting this, we are no better placed to judge the worth of the projects for there is much more to curriculum development than the formulation of aims. It would be like judging the performance of a car from its blueprint.

Another criterion could be that of adoption. If you expected all, or even a large proportion of, schools to adopt the innovations fully then clearly the work of the projects was not worthwhile. However, as we have learned, adoptive aims for dissemination were not necessarily held with much conviction. Indeed, it can be said that a criterion of total adoption is contrary to the current traditions of curriculum control in this country and for this reason any attempt to judge worth by level of uptake or implementation is bound to be hazardous. There is also the question of judging the quality of implementation which merely compounds the problem.

These two examples indicate how difficult it is to judge worth in this context. For this reason I would like to offer a much more simple criterion, the difference between the situation before and after the projects. In this respect there has clearly been a considerable improvement. Today we have available to schools an enormous variety of ideas and materials. There is a heightened awareness and understanding of curriculum matters. Incidental activities have been stimulated by the projects and valuable, if unforeseen outcomes, have ensued. There are Teachers Centres, a more extensive advisory service and other facilities, the provision of which was stimulated by the curriculum development work.

What the curriculum development projects achieved, either directly or indirectly, was primarily the establishment of a facilitating framework for innovation in the schools. I gather that a project, on average, cost around £100,000 at mid-1960s–early 1970s prices for its development phase. This works out roughly at £1,000 for each of the present L.E.A.s, £600 each when there were more of them; and in the case of the Nuffield projects this was met by the Foundation. Such costs for research and development are small. In this respect, there can be little doubt that the work of curriculum development projects *per se* was worth it.

This still leaves us with the question of the worth of the effort in terms of dissemination and implementation. These involve additional and greater costs and considerable personal commitment from administrators, advisers and teachers. Here I believe the evidence indicates that L.E.A.s and their schools gained from a project's work as much as they were prepared to put into supporting and utilizing it. Thus, the extend to which the curriculum innovations can be considered to have been of worth to the schools varies from one part of the country to another. It depended on how much the schools and their L.E.A.s thought it was worth committing effort and resources. In stating this, however, one is alluding merely to one of the simple truths of education. On the whole you get out of it what you are prepared to put into it. The success of curriculum development and implementation was an expression of political priorities and social and personal will. In some cases these were positive and successful, in others ambivalent and negative attitudes led to inactivity.

WHAT ABOUT THE FUTURE?

Our experience of curriculum diffusion over the past decade or so shows that the processes involved in changing the school curriculum are much more sensitive, reactive, changeable and complex than we had antici-pated. Our endeavours had been guided by simple models and theories. These were clearly too limited, too piecemeal and too rigid to offer sufficient guidance in dealing with the reality with which we were faced. It follows that in the future we should develop strategies which are more long-term, holistic and flexible.

A first step in developing new strategies is to accept curriculum development as a continuing and integral part of the educational proc-esses and not to view it as a separated speciality. Whilst it is no doubt true that the input of innovations of recent years has satiated our schools and there is need for a period of calm consolidation, this should not encourage us to direct our efforts elsewhere. The impetus for change tends to come in waves induced by related but broader social and educational movements. The problem is that by the time curriculum changes have been developed, the events that stimulated them have passed; and yet the need for them will still remain. The passing of the pro-science period of the 1960s did not, for example, lessen the need for changes in the curriculum of science education. Motivation now has to come almost exclusively from within the operational arena of the curriculum. This is focussed on the teachers in their classrooms but includes the communication and support, both formal and informal, they can receive within their schools and from outside.

The large-scale curriculum development projects of the 1960s and early 1970s were, in many ways, events of their own time. The national need for curriculum change was accepted with considerable alacrity and, as we have seen, this had a significant impact. If we now lessen our interest in curriculum development it is likely that in a decade or so there will be another call for the same sort of 'big-bang' reaction to events. It will again be the case of 'plus çà change, plus c'est la même chose'! I do not want to suggest that there is no need for large-scale development projects but it does seem to me that we would be better served by a more continuing process of development through adapta-bility; one in which we attempt to anticipate needs and circumstances rather than react to them, and, most importantly, one in which curriculum development and implementation are more closely related.

One reaction against national curriculum development has been a call for school-based curriculum development – the idea being that if teachers undertake development themselves they will be more inspired to implement it adequately and more relevantly to their own situations. There is merit in this view but it has two major drawbacks. The first is economic. Is it reasonable, in terms of resources, for each school to undertake its own work with the consequent large-scale repetition of effort? Do we need to invent the wheel so many times? Second, there is the lack of ideas and inspiration which arises from the isolation of a school. Should not teachers have the benefits of shared experience and the products of work elsewhere?

AREA DEVELOPMENT

Possibly it would be of greatest value to employ strategies of area development in which several schools are involved. They would be associated with an area resource centre which provides physical facilites and supporting personnel enabling teachers to undertake development work co-operatively. In such a system developers and implementers, in effect, are the same people, or, at least, combined together in the same enterprise. As a result at least some of the problems of diffusion, such as those resulting from ambivalence over the aims of dissemination, are reduced. The advantages of school-based curriculum development are provided but more economically, and with the benefits of shared ideas and expertise.

Our diffusion studies revealed a pattern of local activities related to the national projects which arose partly by intent, partly *ad hoc*. These did not necessarily coincide with the boundaries of educational authorities but they represented natural spheres of activity as far as the people involved were concerned. It is such self-forming, self-regulating area groups from which, I suggest, area development should evolve.

Preliminary research in an area will be required to locate the potentially influential key individuals, both official and unofficial, in schools, colleges and elsewhere who can support and stimulate innovation; major communication channels need to be identified; and systems of responsive and flexible decision-making concerned with development and implementation will need to be established. In other words, unlike the situation in the past when diffusion was mainly considered as dissemination after development work was well under way and then purely in terms of formal education structures, I am suggesting we start by discovering the diffusion processes likely to be involved and then design the development and implementation procedures to link with them.

It should also be recognized that the diffusion relationships of curriculum development can also involve people and organizations outside the immediate education community. This is clearly the case when one is developing an aspect of the curriculum, for example, health, environmental or social education, which involves activities outside the school. It is important also for detecting the influences in a community which may affect a curriculum such as the attitudes of parents and other pupils' appreciation of the relevance of a course.

Such strategies will require maintenance in the long-term. This will, of course, be a major task of an area resource centre. In particular it will involve monitoring procedures to provide the information by which development and implementation can be responsive to social and educational change. This will have to be skilfully deployed to counteract the unhelpful negative reactions which will inevitably arise. The pace and variety of development and implementation will need to be regulated and co-ordinated. Also there will need to be encouragement for individual initiatives, acknowledgment of the processes of incidental diffusion, and a sensitivity to the complexity and delicacy of teachers' decision-making in their schools and classrooms. At least in area development there is the possibility of drawing those concerned with curriculum change closer together and so enabling them to appreciate their mutual difficulties and plan ways of overcoming them.

Incidentally, a strategy of area development could lead to undue variety of curricula in the country, although I doubt if this would be much greater than it is at present. However, such variety can, for example, make it difficult for pupils moving from one area to another to relate the different curricula in their old and new schools. For such reasons I suggest that some system for co-ordinating area development is required.

CONTINGENCY RESEARCH

A strategy of area curriculum development would be enhanced by what I would call contingency research. In this we try to answer questions about future possibilities, attempting to determine what would be needed *if* decisions were taken to develop aspects of the curriculum. These can be theoretical questions in that, at the time, there may be no expressed wish for development. The answers to the questions, though, would be based on the realities of the people and circumstances in an area, and could be on offer for when the contingency arises. In that sense the research is anticipatory, offering possibilities to education rather than, as is so often the case in educational research, offering comment on what has been or what is wrong.

Essentially this contingency research would involve a study of curriculum diffusion in the area such as I mentioned earlier. It would be concerned with analyses of the perceptions of teachers, pupils, administrators and the public on curriculum matters; analyses of decision-making and communication; assessments of resources, logistics, manpower use and cost; and the design of strategies of development and implementation appropriate for the area.

In some cases, contingency research could lead to at least small-scale operational studies in which the strategies could be tried out. In this way research would activate practice.

Underlying what I have attempted to say here are two broad ideas. The first is that curriculum development and implementation are parts of a wider process of curriculum diffusion which involves a variety of social and personal behaviour. The particular features of this behaviour are complexity and sensitivity. The second idea is that strategies of development and implementation should be built on an understanding of curriculum diffusion and, within this framework, should attempt to draw the processes of development and implementation as close together as possible. Probably area development linked to contingency research provides the most potent form for such strategies.

These are not new ideas. In fact, in one form or another, they have been proposed by several people in recent years. There have been some experiments with area curriculum development. On a large scale this has, to my knowledge, tended to be short-lived. Teachers Centres, Curriculum Laboratories, and similar organizations in various countries have provided more continuous experiences but, again, I believe this is limited. Further experiments and studies of the way past endeavours have operated, and particularly of their effectiveness in terms of the curriculum needs of the schools, would be most valuable.

Finally, let me emphasize that these ideas are hypotheses. There is no suggestion that they would inevitably be successful. Such a proposition would be most un-*nous*-like. Whether they would work or not depends ultimately on the reasources made available and people's commitment to the ideas. That much, at least, we have learned.

1. P. J. Kelly, *Curriculum Diffusion Research Project Outline Report*, Centre for Science Education, University of London (1975).
2. S. D. Steadman, C. Parsons and B. G. Salter, *An Enquiry into the Impact and Take-up of Schools Council Funded Activities*, Schools Council Publications (1978).
3. P. J. Kelly and R. B. Nicodemus, 'Early stages in the diffusion of the Nuffield A-level biological science project', in *Journal of Biological Education*, VI (1973), 15-22.
4. J. M. Harding, *Communication and Support for Change in School Science Education* (Ph.D. thesis, University of London, 1975).
5. J. M. Harding and P. J. Kelly, 'A study of curriculum diffusion',

in *Journal of the National Association of Inspectors and Educational Advisers*, XVII (1977), 21-31.

6. J. F. Kerr, *Practical Work in School Science* (1963).

7.   For example, P. J. Kelly, 'Evaluation studies of the Nuffield A-level biology trials 2. Evaluation of specific objectives', in *Journal of Biological Education*, VI (1972), 29-40.

6 Action and re-action in science teaching

JIM EGGLESTON

Professor Jack Kerr defined the curriculum as 'all the learning which is planned and guided by the school'.[1] By this definition, the Norwood Committee which reported to the President of the Board of Education in 1941 on *The Curriculum and Examinations in Secondary Schools* found not a curriculum but 'meaningless congeries (of subjects) gathered together (not according to integrating principles which might inform planned learning) but by tradition, chance, pressure or caprice'.[2] The Norwood Committee attacked the problems of the curriculum by proposing changes to the instrumental structure of the education system. They hypothesized needs, grouped pupils according to these needs, and by an unparalleled feat of rationalization, identified three types of mind and gave each its own type of school in which to pursue its distinctive curriculum. They transmuted the School Leaving Certificate and made subject choice, and incidentally early specialization, legitimate. There was nothing in this Report or in the Education Act which followed to cause Black Papers to be written or the Coxes of this world to rise up in defence of standards, with the important exception of the recommendation to make the 16+ examination internal to schools and to give schools responsibility for their own curricula. As we know, this recommendation has not yet been universally accepted by a profession which tends to resist changes in the rules of the instrumental game.

Many potential curricular reforms have been strangled, if not at birth, before they left the breast of the innovator, by the conflicting demands of the selective function imposed on schools.

For me, the main lesson of the Norwood Report and its aftermath is that although changing the administrative structure within which the curriculum functions may be a *necessary* condition for curriculum reform, it is not itself sufficient to ensure it.

What then are these conditions that are both necessary and sufficient to ensure curriculum reform? It is my growing conviction that such conditions will not be defined until we know more about the intellectual and social transactions which attend learning and teaching in our schools. All the informed speculations of philosophers on the nature of knowledge and the investigations of psychologists into the nature of the developing mind are reduced to sophistry in the debate about the curriculum unless their findings are represented in the behaviour of teachers and pupils.

To develop this thesis I intend to examine a spurt of curriculum development in science, in England at the turn of the century, which had much in common with the transatlantic investment in science curriculum reform of more recent times. The catalysts which initiated both these developments were strikingly similar. The ascent of Sputnik I over American skies confirmed a growing suspicion of the superiority of Russian technology. In 1886 Thomas Henry Huxley, defender of Darwin against the onslaughts of Wilberforce, wrote to *The Times*, the inevitable response of the English gentleman to impending doom.

> We have already started upon the most serious struggle for
> existence to which our country has ever been committed . . . The
> latter years of this century promise to see us embark on an
> industrial war of far more serious import than the military wars of
> its opening years. In the East the most systematically instructed and
> best informed people in Europe are our competitors; in the West, an
> energetic offshoot of our own stock, grown bigger than its parent,
> possessed of natural resources to which we can make no pretension,
> and with every prospect of soon possessing that cheap labour by
> which they may be actively utilised.

In both cases a solution to the problem was sought in the educational system and the response to these calls to arms was to examine critically existing science curricula and engage in curriculum reform. In both cases the problems were regarded as too urgent and critical to allow teachers to have a major role in their solution. So we find in America curriculum developers who were professional chemists but amateur educationalists engaged in producing *Chem Study*. In England Professor

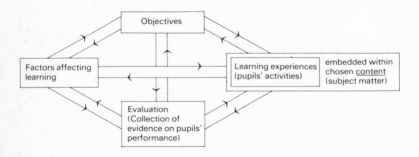

Figure 1. Hilda Taba's curriculum model

Henry E. Armstrong, F.R.S., who always regarded education as too big a job for educationalists, aided and abetted by the British Association for the Advancement of Science, set about the task of reforming the science curricula of schools and other institutions.[3]

In order to elucidate some of the mechanisms of curricula change I will use two schemata, the first due to Hilda Taba,[4] the second a 'home grown' elaborated form of the first which takes into account recent perspectives of students of the curriculum.

TABA'S MODEL

Before educational aims can be more than pious aspirations they require translation from the heady language of poesy to the semantic brass tacks of behavioural terminology. Objectives in this scheme are descriptions of what we expect pupils to learn to do, or to do better. They include both increases in the range and depth of intellectual performance and qualitative and quantitative changes in attitudes.

The domains of cognitive and affective educational objectives have been mapped by Bloom, Krathwohl and others, and need not detain us further here. It is, however, significant that the work of these authors has provided us with a vocabulary and at least the beginnings of organizing principles of a language which facilitates communication about some of the goals of education. There is, as we shall see later, a marked contrast between the language of objectives and the language we use to describe what Taba calls in this scheme learning experiences. In this modification of Taba's scheme, learning experiences are shown as intimately related to content by being embodied in it. Content is the syllabus, the selection of facts and principles made by teachers which, hopefully mediated by learning experiences, will come to be represented in pupils' minds. Content may be selected in order to maximize the likelihood that certain intellectual skills may be developed, certain affective states achieved or to include knowledge which is believed to be important or known to be useful.

The sequence in which content is presented, levels of treatment and the demands made on pupils having learning experiences, necessarily relate to that part of the scheme which is labelled 'factors affecting learning'. The disappointingly meagre offerings of psychologists now include some information on the reasoning processes of the developing mind. Fairly recent work on logical analysis of concepts may soon inform some decisions in the content/learning experiences field. Theories of mind have always played a significant part in the what and how of the curriculum debate. Taba's scheme is completed by an evaluation component which is given a purely empirical significance. It is the acquisition of evidence of pupils' performance on the basis of which we may determine that the objectives of the curriculum have been achieved.

The language used to describe objectives may now limit the activities of evaluators to the short-term achievement of goals which can be measured. Within these limits, the problems of evaluation are technical, concerning the range and precision of data-gathering instruments, and methodological, concerning the design of evaluation studies. It is, however, increasingly recognized that problems of long-term achievement and of unexpected side-effects may demand that the evaluator works on a broader canvas than that of conventional experimental technology.

It is fascinating to delve into the history of science teaching in the 1890s and to use Taba's scheme to examine the progress of Armstrong's attack on the problems of the science curriculum of his time. I am no historian, so I had better explain that this account is based on no more than the published writings of Armstrong and his critics. My perspective is simply that of someone who has been engaged in curriculum development, comparing notes.

OBJECTIVES

We may with advantage extend Taba's scheme to include aims here, as without benefit of Bloom, Armstrong tends to move readily between justifications, aims and objectives. At one point he gives a splendid quotation from Carlyle which, if I read it right, is an early eloquent justification of a position now taken by behavioural psychologists – 'all that man does and brings to pass is the vesture of thought'.[5]

Armstrong held the opinion that 'universal practical teaching of the elements of natural science ... tends to develop a side of the human intellect which is left uncultivated by the most careful literary and mathematical training – the faculty of observing and of reasoning from observations and experiments'.[6] For Armstrong, science was quite unique in that information obtained by the senses, as a result of man's contact with events in the material world, was used both to define and to solve problems. All scientific reasoning started here and knowledge was advanced by manipulating events in the world of objects and phenomena. By an education in science of the kind he advocated quite specific objectives would be achieved. At various points in his writings, he defined the following outcomes which he believed would result from the application of his curriculum.

1. 'The habits of observing accurately, of experimenting exactly with a clearly defined and logical purpose'.[7]
2. 'Logical reasoning from observing and the results of experimental enquiry'.[8]
3. 'Pupils would learn to take nothing for granted'.[9]
4. 'They would learn to devise and fit up apparatus'.[10]
5. 'To devise and carry out experiments'.[11]

6. 'To use a balance and weigh and measure not things only but thoughts and words also'.[12]
7. 'The habit of patiently attending to details is acquired'.[13]
8. 'Encouraged to be properly inquisitive and inquiring'.[14]
9. 'The power of putting questions and obtaining answers by observation and comparison'.[15]
10. 'Imaginative theorizing in practical contexts'.[16]

Sometimes, perhaps inevitably, for one possessed of such reforming zeal, aims were espoused, the achievement of which could hardly be related specifically to science. Such an aim was 'to develop the power of initiative and in all ways to form the character of the pupil'.[17] Armstrong was of the opinion that 'experimental work when properly conducted, affords means of developing the character unquestionably superior to any provided by any other subject in the school curriculum . . . because it touched upon daily practice at every point and on account of its disciplinary value'.[18]

CONTENT

Content is not only the factual content of a syllabus, any more than vocabulary is language. Here content includes the organizing principles by which facts are related to conceptual structures in the mind. In any syllabus there is inevitably a selection of facts from a larger universe of information. The problem of selection is that of articulating the principles on which selection will be based. Recently, conceptual themes which exist at least in the minds of the authors of curriculum materials, have been the main organizing principles. Modern authors tend to provide the pupil with a sort of conceptual Cook's tour of the discipline in which they work. Armstrong's views in these matters were at variance with current practice. He based selection of content on the following principles: (a) syllabus content is selected because of its practical importance to pupils' out-of-school experience; (b) the subject matter of the curriculum must provide a suitable vehicle for the acquisition of skills necessary for practical problem solving.

He was particularly concerned with sequence both of topics in the curriculum and of kinds of intellectual demands made on learners. One can detect themes recently developed in Gagne's work on sequencing and possibly even in Piaget's developmental studies. Armstrong states in one of his essays, 'subjects must be taught in such an order that those which can be treated heuristically (by practical enquiring) shall be mainly attended to in the first instance'.[19] On another occasion he stated 'practical problems must be carefully graduated to the powers of the scholars and they must be insensibly led'.[20] A matter of central concern to Armstrong was that pupils should be aware of the status of the knowledge which they possessed, that they should be able to apply the criteria by which the validity of the facts they learnt could be established: 'the facts must always be so presented to them so that the process by which results are obtained is made sufficiently clear as well as the methods by which any conclusions on these facts are deduced'.[21] The topics which Armstrong included and specifically excluded from the syllabus, which he prepared, make his position abundantly clear. He insisted that, for example, chemistry was to be taught in schools not to produce chemists but to use chemistry as a vehicle for education. His school chemistry course included studies of air, the rusting of iron and the effects of heating food substances, but excluded a study of the oxides of nitrogen which were 'chemists' objects de luxe'. We may infer that Armstrong was less concerned with the development of major conceptual structures in the minds of his students than with chemistry as a vehicle for the exercise of practical problem-solving skills. Perhaps he was more realistic than we are nowadays in his assessment of what pupils can achieve in understanding abstract theories. Indeed, as a professional chemist, Armstrong was critical of all but the best-founded theories. The Ionic theory, which was gaining ground at that time, was singled out for his blistering criticism. Nevertheless, there is evidence that he understood the significance of concepts and the function of a scientific education in fostering their development. He once said of energy, 'no word in the English language carries more meaning to those versed in the principles of physical science, yet how narrow is its connotation in the mind of the uninstructed majority'.[22] Thus it would be wrong to assume, as many critics have done, that the content of Armstrong's science course was based exclusively on practical problem solving.

In 1899, at the British Association meeting at Newcastle upon Tyne, Armstrong read a paper entitled *Suggestions for a Course in Elementary Instruction in Physical Science*.[23] This course included five stages in sequence and spanned the whole of a child's scientific education. The stages are as follows:

1 *Lessons on common familiar objects*. This stage is essentially concrete in its operation. It consists of observing, describing and classifying objects.
2 *Lessons in measurement*. This stage consists of an amalgam of practical arithmetic and elementary physics. It includes a blend of concrete experience and its translation into numbers, coupled with a study of physical properties such as density.
3 *Studies on the effect of heat on things in general; of their behaviour when burnt*.
4 *The problem stage*, including, for example, such problems as to determine what happens when iron rusts; to separate the active

from the inactive constituents of air; to determine what happens when sulphur is burnt, etc.

5 *The quantitative stage.*

6 *Studies of the physical properties of gases in comparison with those of liquids and solids. The molecular and atomic theories and their application.*

LEARNING EXPERIENCE

The word used by Armstrong to describe the learning experiences by which, in his view, science could best contribute to education, was *Heurism*. He defined the term as 'the art of making children discover things for themselves'. The problem of any artist is to communicate his art. So it is with the 'art of teaching'. Recently, Professor Ted Wragg and others of a like mind have been debating the possibility of developing a *science* of teaching. To achieve this it will be necessary to identify and systematize elements of teachers' and pupils' behaviour during the processes of teaching. It is therefore of more than passing interest to find in Armstrong's writings any clues to the process of his heuristic art.

His submission to the Board of Education, published in their special reports, 1899, includes these descriptions.

1 *In general:*
'As far as possible place our students in the attitude of the discoverer'.[24] (Students of education might like to compare this statement with that made by Brunner about 50 years later.)
'A method of teaching which approaches most nearly to the methods of investigation'.[25]
'Students set to solve problems experimentally'; where this is not possible 'the facts must always be so presented to them that the process by which results are obtained is made sufficiently clear, as well as the methods by which any conclusions based on the facts are deduced'.[26]

2 *Pupils:*
'engaged together in work of discovery'. They are encouraged to 'exchange views' and to 'ask each other's advice'.[27]

3 *Teachers:*
'would constantly move about, noting what is being done, criticising and giving brief directions to one group or another'.[28]
'no books will be used but the class would gradually write its own book – when an object has been properly studied – the teacher calls the class together and by judicious questioning will elicit all that is needed for a description of the work done'.[29]

The problem of communicating these prescriptions to teachers, usually untrained and reportedly conditioned to didactic expository teaching in a book-dominated authoritarian climate, was formidable. Indeed Armstrong more than once expressed his sympathy for teachers receiving such communication. One can detect in some of Armstrong's writings about the details of his method a problem well known to modern curriculum developers in scientific subjects. That is, when, in order to communicate the essence of enquiring methods of teaching, an attempt is made to limit the degrees of freedom available to pupils, the result tends to look like a cross between a recipe and a confidence trick.

EVALUATION

The appointment of Mr Hugh Gordon, M.A., to the School Board of London as Science Demonstrator in 1891, was the first step in a succession of events which led to the first ever school-based trials of a curriculum development. Armstrong himself had advocated the application of heuristic methods to heuristic methods – by trial. Formal trials were set up under reasonably controlled conditions in a group of 40 London schools. Later in the longer term uncontrolled attempts were made by more or less well informed teachers to implement heuristic methods. After the London trials, Armstrong was confident that the system 'would prove useful in schools and be most applicable to them'.[30] He stated that this assertion has been 'placed beyond question'[31] as a result of the London trials (though as we will see in a minute, he must have read the report of these trials with rose-tinted spectacles).

By 1927, 30 years later, Armstrong was disillusioned. Westaway, in his influential book on science teaching, rejected heurism as too slow and unworkable. He suspected that Armstrong had never revealed the true secret of his method.

What went wrong?

THE LONDON TRIALS

The British Association curriculum which was largely based on heuristic principles was subjected to trials in 40 London Board schools, under the supervision of Hugh Gordon. Participating teachers were given four kinds of assistance. They were provided with a teacher's guide, *An Elementary Course in Practical Science*, written by Gordon and published by Macmillan. They were supplied with the necessary apparatus, partly by grants of money, but also from a central pool. Some attended a special training course at Berners Street. Gordon (and later Mr Mayhowe Heller, B.Sc., appointed to the project in 1897) visited each school once every two weeks and gave one lesson to each of grades 5, 6 and 7. The demonstrator's visit was described thus by Gordon: 'he would spend a few minutes questioning the class as to the work accomplished during the previous fortnight and dealt with difficulties that had occurred, taking care to emphasise the exact position the experiments already made had left the scholars in; he then invited suggestions as to what would be the next point to elucidate'.[32] Gordon's description further indicates that frequently small groups of boys carried out experiments and demonstrated to the class, thus 'ensuring the closest attention of their fellows'.[33]

Between these fortnightly visits, there were as a rule three intermediate lessons. These were used 'in writing up notes. Also small groups of up to four pupils would perform the chief experiments connected with that portion of the work under consideration'.[34] Even 'writing and composition lessons'[35] might be used for notebook work.

Not all the teachers involved in his trials had attended the training course and unwittingly Gordon had something like an educational experiment on his hands. Admittedly teachers were not assigned at random to be trained or not trained and no measures of achievement were used. But Gordon's observations within these obviously severe limitations are interesting and possibly not without significance. For the trained group he commented on experimental work, 'that a living interest in what was going on was aroused which was reflected in the subsequent work of the class'.[36] The responses of the classes taught by trained teachers to the demonstrator's invitation to consider the next point to elucidate was that 'very good suggestions were often made, but as a rule the class had to be led to the consideration of the next question to be answered'.[37]

He reported on the untrained groups thus, 'perhaps at first unwilling to take the trouble involved in keeping the boys at experimental work, it often happened that the class lost interest and the results were unsatisfactory'.[38] It is surprising that Armstrong, so skilled in inference, so dedicated to the critical examination of evidence, should fail to appreciate the implications of Gordon's evidence, impressionistic though it was.

DID THE HEURISTIC METHOD FAIL?

Most commentators since Armstrong's time have concluded that it did. Speculations about the cause of its failure range from the plausible to those which stem from a gross misunderstanding of the method. The factors which determine the survival or evolution of a curriculum may be more complex than those represented in the 'model' derived from Taba and represented in figure 1. Successive attempts at curriculum development have been accompanied by a growing awareness of the complexity of the curriculum process and a broadening of the conceptual base for evaluation. I have tried to indicate some of the more significant

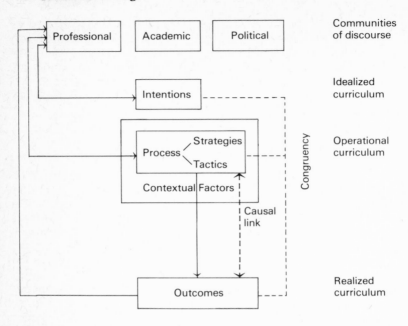

Figure 2. Diagram to illustrate some functional links in evaluation of a curriculum

developments of our understanding of the process of curriculum development in figure 2.

It would appear that *objectives* described with the precision of behavioural terminology represent a sub-set of the set *intentions*. The latter will include not only facts and principles to be learnt, cognitive operations to be practised and affective states to be achieved, but also a map of concepts which provide the structural framework which give facts meaning. Also the selection of facts and concepts to be learnt will be derived rationally from explicit statements of goals. The substance, and the form of knowledge to be transmitted as well as the methods for its validation are all legitimate candidates for inclusion in the set *intentions*.

Similarly 'learning experiences' which may have been considered to be determined by curriculum materials in the first optimistic flush of national curriculum developments, are now known to be subject to phenotypical variation due to the 'effects' of teachers and the school contexts in which they operate. The observed, operational curriculum, is the result of decisions made by teachers. These decisions may be strategic or tactical. Strategic implies decisions taken before the event (course of lessons or a single lesson) about the form the lesson will take, the resources to be used and the method of their deployment. Tactics suggests blow-by-blow interactions, the script of the lesson 'written' by the participants as the lesson proceeds, for example the kinds of questions a teacher asks and the nature of teacher interventions in pupil-pupil or pupil-resource interactions.

When evaluation is designed to achieve more than the summative judgment 'were the objectives achieved?' and when its function is to give an account of the mechanisms of the curriculum, the congruency between intentions and the strategies and tactics adopted by teachers becomes highly significant. In the case of Armstrong's *Elementary Course in Practical Science*, the account given by Hugh Gordon of the London Trials indicates a lack of congruence between the intentions articulated in Armstrong's published writings and the strategies (and possibly tactics) used by at least some teachers. Perhaps 'heurism' failed to be implemented rather than failed when implemented. In the *Journal of Education* (1925) Armstrong[39] conceded that his 'heuristic method' for teaching science had failed, possibly, as he put it, due to 'the implastic nature of human materials; that no single system of education could cope with the wide range of social class, sex, age, and ability present in our schools'. This conclusion seems to direct attention to those contextual factors which set limits to the range of strategies and tactics which can be used in curriculum processes, as well as restricting intentions to those in harmony with the social and intellectual climate of the times. I would speculate that 'the heuristic method' applied to science teaching in schools in the late nineteenth century was at variance both with the intellectual climate in science, which was increasingly dominated by theory building, and the social function of the educational system, which was concerned with upward social mobility. Science's claim to a place in the secondary schools curriculum, particularly in grammar schools, was not universally accepted. It may be that the 'practical problem solving', a theoretical stance of Armstrong's course, as well as its potential cost in terms of workshops and apparatus, made it uncongenial to headmasters and governors. Again the examinable products of 'heuristic learning' were alien to the scholarly ethos of school courses in such disciplines as history, Latin and mathematics. The schools curriculum exists in a homeostatic relationship with social values and aspirations.

Referring again to the diagram we note the correspondence between, in Taba's figure-evaluation, the collection of evidence of pupils' performance, and *outcomes* in figure 2. The latter term is meant to convey the collection of data on any significant change in pupil behaviour, which may or may not be consistent with intentions, i.e. it includes unexpected benefits and undesirable side effects as well as intended effects. The latter may be observed. However, to establish that processes found to be congruent with intentions are *causally* linked with any outcome intended or otherwise is an empirical question. The hypothesis that defined processes cause observable effects can be tested only by experimental and correlational methods. In the case of Armstrong's *Elementary Course in Practical Science* such hypotheses were not rigorously tested. Even though the trials described by Hugh Gordon seem to indicate that circumstances existed to conduct at least a correlational study, I have found no evidence to suggest that outcomes were systematically observed and related to processes. We do not know, so far as I am aware, if during the London trials Armstrong's intentions were achieved even under conditions deemed to be propitious.

The articulation of *intentions*, the definition of *processes* in order to establish congruence between them and the systematic observation of *outcomes* in order to examine hypothetical causal links with processes, may be considered to be intrinsic evaluative methods. However, the survival of curriculum developments may be determined by factors *external* to the development process. Schools, teachers and children, the human agencies of the curriculum, and the substance and form of the schools' curriculum relate to communities outside the school. Three communities of discourse whose knowledge and values have considerable influence on the curriculum have been identified in figure 2.

Forms of knowledge identified with academic disciplines are the particular concern of the academic community. Each discipline is identified with a body of facts, conceptual structures which give these facts form and meaning, and with methods of enquiry which add to the store of facts and elaborate explanatory theories. The apparatus of dissemination, publication, teaching and examining provide the means whereby the disciples come to share common knowledge, concepts and theories, and try to secure agreement on methods of enquiry and subscribe to common values. The community can and does exert a powerful influence on the school's curriculum. It may be that Armstrong's manifesto for science education with its emphasis on practical problem solving and its de-emphasis on theory was at variance with the perception of the academic community of his day of the function of science in the schools' curriculum.

Teachers comprise the professional community of discourse. The operational curriculum, no matter who defined intentions, is in their hands. Therefore the perceptions which teachers develop of the nature of knowledge, of the minds of their pupils and the purposes of schooling will critically determine the chances of survival of any curriculum innovation. The demands made on science teachers by Armstrong's heuristic methods may have been beyond their competence or too remote from their priorities. Science teachers, indeed the sciences as disciplines, had not yet achieved the status of academic responsibility afforded to classics or mathematics. Moreover, the schools' climate was authoritarian and bookish, increasingly dominated by inflexible examinations. It is not surprising that in such circumstances a prescription for science teaching which eschewed the text book and gave teachers the job of stage managers rather than the title role in classroom interactions received less than universal support.

Finally, the political community of discourse may exert a significant influence on the survival chances of the curriculum development. It is of more than passing interest that Armstrong's motives were in a sense political. His conviction that commercial enterprise could only be sustained by a breed of men with practical problem-solving skills and the initiative and confidence to exercise them in pursuit of solutions to industrial problems should have commended itself to those who provide the financial resources to maintain schools. Parents also might have supported proposals to provide a curriculum which potentially fitted their sons for key industrial posts. The political community did not however rally to the support of Armstrong's cause. Historians no doubt may resolve this problem but I regret, having neither the time nor resources, I must leave this issue to them.

1. J. F. Kerr (ed.), *Changing the Curriculum* (1968).
2. Norwood Report, Board of Education, *Curriculum and Examination in Secondary Schools*, Report of the Committee of Secondary School Examinations Council, 1941 (published H.M.S.O. 1943).
3. H. E. Armstrong, 'The place of research in education and of science in industry', in H. E. Armstrong, *The Teaching of Scientific Methods* (1903), 124.
4. H. Taba, *Curriculum Development Theory and Practice* (New York, 1962), 309.
5. H. E. Armstrong, *Address to the Educational Science Section of the British Association for the Advancement of Science, Belfast* (1902).
6. H. E. Armstrong, 'On the teaching of natural science as part of the ordinary school course and on the method of teaching chemistry in the introductory course in science classes', *Schools and Colleges, International Conference on Education* (1884). (Quoted in W. H. Brock, *H. E. Armstrong and the Teaching of Science*, 1973).
7. H. E. Armstrong, 'The teaching of scientific method', in *The Education Times* (May 1891).
8. H. E. Armstrong, 'The heuristic method of teaching and the art of making children discover things for themselves', in *Board of Education, Special Reports on Educational Subjects*, vol. 2 (1898).

9. Armstrong, *The Teaching of Scientific Methods*, op. cit., 257.
10. *Ibid.*
11. *Ibid.*
12. *Ibid.*
13. *Ibid.*
14. *Ibid.*
15. H. E. Armstrong, 'Training in scientific methods as a central motive in elementary schools' (Report of Conference at Guildford, June, 1902), reproduced in *The Teaching of Scientific Methods*, op. cit.
16. Inferred from Armstrong's *B.A. Address, Belfast*, 1902. See Armstrong, *The Teaching of Scientific Methods*, op. cit., 41-2.
17. Armstrong, 'The heuristic method', op. cit.
18. Armstrong, *The Teaching of Scientific Methods*, op. cit., 255.
19. *Ibid.*
20. Armstrong, *The Teaching of Scientific Methods*, op. cit., 254.
21. *Ibid.*, 255.
22. Armstrong's *B.A. Address*, op. cit., 46.
23. H. E. Armstrong, 'Suggestions for a course of elementary instruction in physical science', in *Report on Teaching Chemistry, B.A. Meeting, Newcastle upon Tyne* (1889).
24. Armstrong, *The Teaching of Scientific Methods*, op. cit., 236.
25. *Ibid.*, 237.
26. *Ibid.*, 241 and 255.
27. *Ibid.*, 259.
28. *Ibid.*, 260.
29. *Ibid.*, 244.
30. *Ibid.*
31. *Ibid.*
32. H. Gordon and M. Heller, Appendix C to Armstrong's *The Teaching of Scientific Methods*, op. cit.
33. *Ibid.*
34. *Ibid.*
35. *Ibid.*
36. *Ibid.*
37. *Ibid.*
38. *Ibid.*
39. H. E. Armstrong, 'Future science of the schools', in *Journal of Education* (1925). See Brock, op. cit.

7 Curriculum change: product or process?

PAT D'ARCY

It may not have been the intention of the researchers funded by the Schools Council, and the Nuffield and Ford Foundations in the mid-1960s and early 1970s, but to teachers in schools or at in-service conferences, what was on offer must have seemed very product-oriented. 'Resources for Learning' were mainly booklets and worksheets whether they came from Projects for Science or Humanities or Integrated Studies or General Studies or whatever.

I know, from personal experience, that the intention behind many of these materials was to change teaching methods as well as means. I recall, for instance, the controversy (sometimes heated) that the 'neutral chairman' concept provoked when it was suggested as a way of presenting materials from the Schools Council Humanities Project: all those video-taped lessons showing the teacher gazing round the group waiting for the students to inform each other of their opinions . . . There were also the earnest discussions that went on about the best structure for a worksheet: should it allow the student to find his own answers or should it programme him firmly along the correct path towards the 'right' answer?

So there was certainly discussion outside the classroom about how to deal with all these new materials most effectively, but in spite of this, the main changes inside the classroom were to do with products. In that golden age when money was more readily available than it is to day, worksheets, film strips, booklets, pictures, posters, cassette tapes and O.H.P.s proliferated! Many of us have since realized that it is much easier to change materials than to change methods. There is no real problem (apart from funds) about provision and on the whole no objection to it either; we all enjoy being given things. But when these presents involve changing classroom behaviour, either the pupils' or the teacher's, then they tend to be regarded with suspicion.

If, however, curriculum change is to involve changes in how learning happens as well as in what is learnt, then it *must* be about changes in pupil and teacher behaviour as well as in the materials they are working with. In fact I see the loss of faith in materials to do the job on their own not as a regression but as a step forward. We are now realizing as we approach the 1980s that more dynamic and fundamental changes are going to be necessary if learning is to become more effective for more children.

I believe that these further changes that we need to make are mostly to do with process – or processes. We need to find out more about how learning or mental growth or intellectual development occurs before we can make full use of all the materials that are now available. Similarly at the 'out-put' end of the classroom, I am convinced that we would do better to be less product-oriented, less concerned to test and to measure, more ready to accept that students are still learning at the end of their fifth, sixth or seventh year in secondary education – and are not in any way at a quantifiable end point.

This is not to imply that we should not be concerned to obtain as detailed a picture as we can of a student's progress. How can we help in further development unless we are aware on the one hand of the understanding that he already possesses and on the other of the obstacles which lie in his path? One of my quarrels with the present system of examining and assessing is that it does not seek to map out a detailed picture for each student. Instead the teacher/examiner sets up his own obstacle race and judges the student's performance on that course alone!

What I would like to do in this paper is to describe how my increasing 'process consciousness' has influenced my expectations and my responses to pupils' work in the classroom. It will be clear from my illustrations that I am an English teacher but I am sure that a similar paper could be written from the same principles and with much the same implications by a teacher of any other subject.

To start with the syllabus – or rather to start with my reluctance to produce a syllabus when I became the head of an English department in a secondary modern school 'going comprehensive' in the mid-1970s. I did not want to lay down what was to be taught in the first year, the second year and so on or what was to be expected in the way of products from every child at the end of a particular year. I felt uneasy about stipulating that every pupil should or would be able to use full stops consistently by the age of 12, speech marks by the age of 12½, semi-colons by the age of . . .? I also felt uneasy about specifying amounts of time to be spent on reading, talking, writing, listening or the exact books that should be used to encourage any of these activities.

It seemed to me to be more important to be explicit about the criteria or the philosophy that I hoped would influence the teaching of everyone in the department and along with it the learning of every pupil who came to us for English lessons. In other words, I believed that a clear idea of objectives would be more influential than a clear ruling about what books should be used or which punctuation marks taught.

The first paper that I wrote for the department had 20 points in it; I quote the first 10 here to give some idea of what I mean by the difference between a syllabus and a statement of aims and objectives. In my second year in the department, I produced a kind of intermediary document which currently Heads like to refer to as a 'scheme of work' which outlined, in rather more detail, themes which would be 'reserved' for each year group to avoid overkill with some and total neglect of others, but I still believe that if the criteria quoted here are adhered to, then nothing much will go amiss whatever the materials that are offered by the teacher to the group. This then is the text of that first departmental paper:

PAPER ONE

a I have called this paper 'A Language Policy for Learning' because I believe that language and learning are inextricable. They do not develop separately and cannot be taught separately.

b Similarly, the four modes of language: talking, listening, reading and writing need to interlock if each is to develop in any permanent sense of the word 'development'.

c At the root of language and learning development is thinking – and it is above all else to the opportunities created in English lessons for different kinds of thinking, that attention and effort should be given.

d I believe that fundamentally education is about the development of thought processes – because the sense that we make of the world and our own relation to it depends ultimately on how we are able to think.

e We should therefore be more concerned with developing children's capacities to probe experience thoughtfully than with their ability to retain information only in the short term in order to be able to regurgitate it in fairly low-level examinations.

f Recollecting, reflecting, selecting, connecting, interpreting, analysing, speculating, imagining . . . we should ask ourselves continually whether the work we have been requiring from children involves any of these mental activities. We should seek constantly to extend the range and to sustain the play of thought backwards and forwards across this spectrum.

g Talking, listening, reading and writing are all crucial language modes through which such thinking activities can happen. This is true across all subjects on the curriculum although our specific concern here is with the English department.

h At the heart of any English work should be a concern for and a genuine interest in the individual student. We have in my view, an enormous advantage over almost every other department in this respect. We have no set syllabus of information to teach – our job is to encourage the individual to use language to help him to clarify his own experience and thereby to clarify his sense of himself and of ways in which he can relate to other people.

i I believe that this focus is equally central to literature and that when we are deflected from it towards a consideration of form divorced from feeling, we are doing a major disservice to any writer who has felt sufficiently strongly about human experience to give it a shape in a novel or a poem or a play.

j If we accept (h) and (i) then the need to activate the student's own thoughts and feelings is paramount. Whenever we fail to do this, he is performing – if at all – in a 'cut off' kind of way which will never have any permanent effect on the way he sees either the world or himself.

It will be clear from this half of my first Paper for the department that my over-riding concern was that we should all recognize the inter-relatedness of language (whatever the mode) with thinking and learning. We still fall too easily into the trap of assuming that reading and writing can be taught – and tested – in isolation from the thinking which the individual reader or writer is able or willing to engage in and from the point that he or she has reached in the process of learning about this topic or that. I cannot understand, for instance, how so many teachers are ready to accept statements about a child's reading age (arrived at as the result of performance on a specific test) as though this figure were an absolute which allowed for generalizations about the reading ability of that child in *any* reading situation.

If, on the other hand, we regard the development of language and thought and learning as continually interdependent and continually on the move, perhaps we can imagine it as a double helix which generates further links in the spiralling chain as thought generates language which in turn leads to learning which in turn produces fresh thoughts, fresh insights and fresh formulations. If we believe education to be about that kind of growth, then it stands to reason that our activities in school must allow for that kind of growth to happen. Which brings me back once again, to the difference between *product* and *process*, between *reproduction* and *reconstruction*.

In a product-oriented classroom, the teacher usually provides what is to be taught, for how long and with what outcome. It is essentially a 'feed in, fill up, feed out' model of learning which seeks evidence for what has been learnt in the ability of the student to reproduce what the teacher had in mind as the outcome from the start. For such a class situation, the teacher has no difficulty in drawing up a set syllabus or in specifying what skills or what knowledge the students should have acquired by the end of the term. Unfortunately, many students (in top streams as well as bottom) fail to demonstrate the reliability of those expectations in both internal and external examinations.

This is another cogent reason in my view for changing the emphasis from product to process. In a process-oriented classroom the teacher makes fewer decisions and allows more choice of topic and activities to individual students. In consequence, the programme is less structured in the sense that it cannot be specified beforehand. It is also less predictable because outcomes are not pre-designed in the teacher's mind. As a teaching model it is more concerned with *reconstruction* than *reproduction*, accepting to a much greater extent the part that must be played in new thinking, learning and language development by the student's own previous experiences. The inside of the student's head if you like is perceived by the teacher as a space already populated by many images which only the student can interpret in their relation to each other, not an *empty* space into which the teacher will project his own fully-formed picture.

I would like to add at this point that I am more and more convinced that we continually under-rate the power of our students' minds, whatever their so-called 'level of ability'. By ignoring their own potential and constantly seeking to focus their attention *outwards* onto other people's thinking, we deny them a sense of wonder and excitement in the ability of their own brain to make meaning which often puts them off thinking and learning and making their own formulations for life.

Ann Berthoff[1] in a book called *Forming, Thinking, Writing* puts it like this when she is reflecting on how students learn to write:

> You don't have to philosophize or master psychological theories
> in order to learn to write, but it's important and I think comforting
> to know that the means of making meaning which you depend on
> when you make sense of the world and when you write, are in
> part made for you by your brain and by language itself.

It took me five terms back in school before I gained the confidence to make a major commitment of time to this process-oriented way of working. I had talked a lot to my students about the need to think for themselves about what they read, or watched on television, or wrote about and I had responded to what they wrote in what I hoped was a thoughtful and supportive way. I had tried to provide what we had described in the Writing Across the Curriculum Project[2] as a 'partner in dialogue' audience whenever possible.

Then, at the beginning of the second summer term, I came back from a conference of primary and secondary teachers interested above all in child-centred learning and I felt so heartened by what I had heard, that

I 'gave' my third and fourth year groups all their English lessons for the whole of that term to plan their own work and make their own choices.

I had prepared a detailed booklet (I still could not entirely shake off a belief that materials were necessary!) which gave plenty of suggestions for talking, reading, tape recording and writing – it was barely glanced at by either group. Even when they ran out of ideas, they never seemed to get started again very successfully from mine, a point I still puzzle over.

However, there was no shortage of ideas from most pupils and work in English lessons got under way with considerably more drive than previously. Please notice, it was not a new set of books, or my specially made booklet, or indeed any 'in-put' of that kind which stimulated these boys and girls (supposedly of average ability and below) to make an effort – and much more importantly perhaps, which sustained their interest and led to new initiatives throughout that term and on into the next. It was their discovery, from being given the opportunity to do it, that they could very happily make their own choices, especially when these were taken seriously for an extended length of time and not just given lip service at the end of term or when the teacher ran out of ideas. What is more, the words they put onto paper made sense in a way which satisfied them, satisfied me, and motivated them to further efforts.

I would like to quote at some length from the work of two students who were then in their fourth year, partly because it will make a refreshing change from my own writing and partly because I would like to show how it is possible to respond to student writing analytically rather than evaluatively. I never gave grades even in the fifth year, and although this was unusual in the school, I was never pressed to do so either by students or parents. If they could not read my handwriting though, students would invariably come and ask me what I had said in the five or six lines of writing at the end of a piece of work.

Anyway, here is the opening of a very long, thoughtful and informative piece that Dougal wrote about Bardsey Island, where he had spent many summer holidays with his family. As far as I remember, he started writing it before Whitsuntide and using most of his homework time as well as time in class, finished the piece (30–40 pages) by the end of term.

BARDSEY ISLAND
My face is grimacing from the lump in my stomach caused by the long drive from home.
The boat is old and wooden but large and safe, its bows ride high on the glistening sea.
The headland is well out to sea and it conceals the familiar shape of the island, the mainland coast passes by slowly, shear rocks plunge

into the sea, tiny inaccessible beaches look cold without the people and hubbub.

I imagine what it will be like when we come around below the islands mountain and see the little pebble beach with its slipway and the rickety boathouse on the bank above.

The bearded figure at the head of the boat guides it out past the floats and corks which mark lobster pots, each one placed as it has been for years, each one as emptey as the fishermans pockets.

The Bows of the boat are angled out to clear the headland, which is still a long way off.

The tops of the mainland cliffs merge into grass and heather and then into ferns and prickly yellow gorse bushes.

I wonder whether there will be anyone waiting for us, If there was I probably wouldn't recognise them.

I spot the top of the Mountain above the tapering peninsula and wait for its intirity to appear and warm my cold skin; as it appears, it appears to be low in the water and a long way across the choppy water of the sound.

Boldly the boat heads out and begins to heave against the swirling under currents; the island grows until the mountain looms over the sea like a spider, it shrouds the cliffs and rocks which are home for birds, fish and seals.

The boat is steered into the shelter of the Mountain and around it into the lowland Cafu the otherside, again lobster pots and floats have to be avoided, if the propeller gets caught up in the ropes, the danger of currents and the lifeless rocks will be strong.

Excitement grows as a figure is spotted on the shaded mountain, guesses are made as to who it is, but whoever it is, we wave and smile.

Around the mountain the south end appears, stretching out into the Irish sea, the lighthouse appears as I had imagined it, its tower painted boldly with Red and white. The narrow harbour is edged by wet and glistening rocks some of which are accompanied by wary gulls.

The boat slows and pulls into the narrow shelter, two fishermen hold the boat while boxes sacks and containers, are unloaded.

Everyone chats about how long its been and how we've all changed, while all I want to do is get up to the house, our beautiful house with its well and ty bach (outside toilet).

When I first read these opening pages I was immediately impressed by the interplay of thought and feeling and I started to write in the margin all the different kinds of thinking that I could detect. Up to the short paragraph beginning 'I wonder whether there will be anyone waiting for us' I had jotted in the margin 'recording, recollecting, interpreting, imagining, generalising, observing, speculating'. I then asked Dougal to read through what he had written and to continue annotating the various processes which had been involved. I thought that he would be interested to reflect in this way on what he had written. (How often do we ask students to comment seriously on their own work?) For the rest of the passage that is in print here he added 'observing, connecting, factualising, noting, wondering, happiness, excitement and impatience'. Over the Bardsey piece as a whole (which would have printed into a very readable and interesting booklet given the time and the reprographic resources to do it) Dougal had certainly used writing for a wide variety of purposes – to inform, to re-shape his own past experiences, to reflect and to speculate about the future of the island. It included writing that was transactional, expressive and poetic as well as some carefully drawn sketches and maps. Throughout, Dougal was at the centre of what he was writing, whichever of these purposes was dominant, and I am sure that this was what motivated him to sustain the effort of putting it into words so effectively and at such length.

Michael chose at some stage in that same summer term to start writing about the summer of the previous year – when he had worked as a glass collector at a sea-side pub on a huge caravan site. He started writing down his memories in rough – it all looked very scrawly and messy and for a long time he wouldn't let me read what he was writing. 'Wait till I've written it out neatly.' I began to think that he never would, but by the end of the term he had half filled a notebook with a second draft all beautifully written out in black ink. When I read this I was so excited by the quality of the perceptions that he was making that I could hardly wait to see the rest. I saw no more until nearly the end of the following term when the completed piece was finally handed in. Here is a passage from the second notebook; it is part of a long section in his recollections where a group of lads who come to the site every year for their fortnight's holiday end their stay with a (by now) traditional beer fight:

THE BEER FIGHT
Soon the floor was flooded with beer which made me want to cry, all that beer wasted I contemplated getting a straw and drinking it all though it seemed a little outrageous at the time. After everyone had finished expressing their childishness which is not a bad thing, (I do so by making sandcastles) the clearing up operation had to start. The bouncers who were also employed during the daytime when the pub was busy, ensured that the lads didn't leave, it was their job to clear the mess up though they seemed to further the mess by doing so. They found the beer made the floor quite a good

skating rink so quite a while was spent discovering their unknown flair for ice skating, sorry beer skating. The mops and buckets provided for the clearing up job were rather misused and their rather unorthodox method of cleaning up provided many a laugh amongst themselves though the joke had gone a little too far for the manager's likeing. Eventually they were allowed to leave, there was then an arguement between the cleaners and the managers who demanded more pay for having to clear the mess up, it was quickly granted due to the pub having to open in two hours time. The managers debated as to whether the lads should be banned or not though they never were, too much trade would be lost. As the cleaners, fag in mouth, dirty overall, hole in tights category, attempted to clear the floor of beer and drenched beer mats they made various suggestions as to why the lads did this disgusting act. They blamed the parents then the schools then their mentality then came to the conclusion that it was just the society of today, it would never of happened in their days. During the ritual fight the managers always falsely threatened to call the police, in an attempt to deter the lads though they knew it was only a bluff due to the same threat being made every year. The fight became yet another occasion that I will remember in my year as a glass collector, it was rather pathetic but it was fun.

The next day the lads left, though before doing so they had a farewell pint while singing rather more nostalgic songs which matched their mood. They gave a meaningful kiss to their departing girl friends an apology to the managers and as they left gave a burst of song and a wave to the bar staff and myself in appreciation of our work. All was forgiven no one held any grudges against them, their departure meant the pub would now be dead, that happy feeling they radiated was gone though it would soon be back. Alright so you've seen it all in the movies but when it happens in real life it makes you want to cry. It was the first year I'd ever known the New Tredegar lads which is probably why they had such an impact on me. I suppose after seeing them year after year they become part of the furniture no longer something new and different no more a contrast, but are just taken for granted. I wanted to be associated with them part of their happiness and when one of them spoke to me I felt as if they recognised me which made me feel good. The situation is much the same at school. I am a well known figure just like the lads were and I find that many first second and third years want to know me and be able to say that I am a friend of theirs. I know this due to them constantly saying hello to me and making what their age group see as funny jokes they look up to me and want to be associated with the so called big boy of the fifth year as I did with the New Tredegar lads. I still remember those people I used to idolise when at school they've long forgotten me as I will forget those kids who idolise me just as I will always remember the New Tredegar lads and they will forget me. Hopefully someday in later life I'll be a prominent figure and people will look up to me, at least I know how they feel and will try to remember them.

The lads were a good laugh although at times they got slightly out of hand, they made many people smile which is a nice thing to be able to do.

Not only can Mike create a vivid picture of the scene, he can also generalize about it, and interpret other people's motives. As he reflects in retrospect on his own feelings, the role reversal that he is able to make towards the end is full of insights which appear to reveal themselves to him as he writes. This whole piece illustrated powerfully for me the truth of William Stafford's comment: 'A writer is not so much someone who has something to say as he is someone who has found a process that will bring about new things he would not have thought of if he had not started to say them.'

Another Schools Council Project,[3] whose report is published this year, has come to the conclusion after several years of observation and analysis that the most important factor which enables a student to draw meaning from any text is his *willingness to reflect on what he is reading*. In my classroom last year, I have absolutely no doubt that by shifting the emphasis from product to process I had managed to encourage that 'willingness to reflect' which in its turn, produced writing of a far more thoughtful and perceptive nature than any I had previously encountered from the group. Other teachers making similar shifts of emphasis have experienced very similar results notably, from evidence in print, Ken Macrorie[4] in the USA and Michael Armstrong in this country.[5]

In the passages just quoted, I think it is clear that for both these pupils *real* learning had taken place. If the aim of future curriculum change is to facilitate similar experiences then a closer consideration of how such learning happens must be undertaken. So much of the existing material emphasizes the separate roles of the teachers and pupils as the givers and receivers of knowledge. A first step in the right direction would therefore be any attempt which seeks to close this gap between teachers and learners and which emphasizes the importance of their reflecting together on what has been happening in the classroom. This would require both parties engaged in the learning experience to make joint decisions about where to go next, based on a careful and considered reflection of the work currently in progress.

Future curriculum development should therefore be less concerned about the nature of specific content; rather it should place more emphasis on the study of the classroom process. Above all it follows that any evaluation concerned solely with monitoring products by testing discrete items of performance, currently being encouraged by way of record cards and item banking systems, will at best be inadequate and at worst positively damaging. There needs to be much more serious acknowledgment of the need for an individual context to any comment about a pupil's 'performance'.

Too many previous attempts at curriculum change have sought to impose ideas from outside the classroom on those inside, chiefly by prescribing the outcomes to be measured. As presented here the curriculum is something organic and grows over the course of the school year as both pupils and teachers attempt to match the problems and the progress that each partner in the enterprise has noticed in the work tackled together. I see this approach as preferable to a model of curriculum development which seeks to evaluate change in pupils by making arbitrary 'measurements' of arbitrary 'answers' to arbitrary 'questions'.

1. Ann Berthoff, *Forming, Thinking, Writing* (New Jersey, 1978).
2. Martin, D'Arcy, *Writing and Learning* (1976).
3. Schools Council Report, *The Effective Use of Reading Project* (1979).
4. Ken Macrorie, *Uptaught* (New Jersey, 1970); *idem, A Vulnerable Teacher* (New Jersey, 1974).
5. Michael Armstrong, *Closely Observed Children* (1979).

Details of contributors

Pat D'Arcy has worked for two Schools Council Projects, 'Reading for Meaning' and 'Writing across the Curriculum'. She has worked in every kind of secondary school: grammar, secondary modern and comprehensive – traditional, liberal and middle of the road. She was Chairman of the National Association for the Teaching of English from 1976–8 and she works at present as a County English Adviser for Wiltshire.

Jim Eggleston is Professor of Education at Nottingham University. After 12 years teaching biology he resigned his post as Head of Science at Hinckley Grammar School to serve an apprenticeship in Educational Research under Professor J. F. Kerr. Later he was appointed to the staff of the School of Education at the University of Leicester. He co-directed the School Council sponsored project on the Evaluation of Science Teaching Methods before taking up his present post at Nottingham.

Maurice Galton taught chemistry in schools and at University level before coming to Leicester in 1970 to work as a Research Fellow on the Schools Council project for the Evaluation of Science Teaching Methods directed by Professor Kerr and Professor Eggleston. He is now a senior Lecturer in the Education Department and co-director of a major programme of research seeking to evaluate the effectiveness of different teaching styles in the primary school.

Paul Hirst is Professor of Education in the University of Cambridge. After teaching mathematics in secondary schools for some years he held lectureships at the University of Oxford and the University of London Institute of Education. From 1965–71 he was Professor of Education at King's College, London. He has been much involved with recent developments in the philosophy of education, writing particularly on the theory of knowledge and the curriculum. He was a contributor to the original series of public lectures on the curriculum that followed Professor Kerr's inaugural at the University of Leicester in 1967.

Peter Kelly is Professor of Education, Head of the Department and Dean of the Faculty of Educational Studies at Southampton University. Previously he was Professor of Biological Education at the Centre for Science Education at Chelsea College in the University of London and from 1972–5 directed the Curriculum Diffusion Research Project there. His association with Professor Kerr goes back to the 1960s when they were both deeply involved with curriculum development projects in science education.

David Tomley was a trials teacher of both the Nuffield O-level and A-level biology courses while at the Manchester Grammar School. More recently he was area co-ordinator and author for the Nuffield Working with Science Project where he first became involved with Professor Kerr. He worked in a College of Education before joining the staff of Leicester University where he is a lecturer in education in charge of one of the two main sections of the post-graduates certificate course.

Richard Whitfield is Professor of Education, Head of the Department of Educational Enquiry and Dean of the Faculty of Social Sciences and Humanities at the University of Aston in Birmingham. He studied part-time for the Leicester M.Ed. degree by research under Professor Kerr's supervision from 1965 to 1968, and was on the staff of the University of Cambridge Department of Education for several years before moving to Aston in 1975.

Index